T

Robert Schumann

Editor

Karl Storck

Alpha Editions

This edition published in 2020

ISBN : 9789354008535

Design and Setting By
Alpha Editions
email - alphaedis@gmail.com

THE LETTERS OF ROBERT SCHUMANN

SELECTED AND EDITED BY DR. KARL STORCK

TRANSLATED BY HANNAH BRYANT

LONDON
JOHN MURRAY, ALBEMARLE STREET, W.
1907

CONTENTS

BOOK I

STURM UND DRANG

PART I

JEAN PAUL AND DRYASDUST

PART II

FLORESTAN AND EUSEBIUS

PART III

THE 'DAVIDSBÜNDLER'

BOOK II

THE FIGHT FOR CLARA

BOOK III

AT THE ZENITH

APPENDIX

PREFACE

'There are many to proclaim
Klopstock's fame;
There are fewer who could quote
What he wrote.
Such grandeur's little gain
To attain;
For myself I choose instead
To be read.'

If Lessing's pessimistic epigram is justified with regard to poetry, it may with equal truth be applied to the indifference commonly displayed towards the letters of eminent persons, and particularly towards musicians' letters, which so seldom possess a purely literary interest. It was my conviction of this which led me to bring out the present selection of Schumann's letters, and the earlier volumes on Beethoven and Mozart. A man's letters undoubtedly form one of the best clues to his character; but while the student will welcome almost any number of these documents in the hope of gaining insight into the writer's mind, there must be many music-lovers who have neither time nor opportunity for such researches, and it is for them, primarily, that this volume has been compiled.

There was little difficulty in making an attractive selection in Schumann's case, for his letters have a considerable literary value. I have, further, so arranged them as to form something of a biography, with the idea of providing a picture of Schumann's inner development, as well as of his outward career. To this picture the introductory chapters provide a frame, and some explanatory notes have been added.

For this book I have drawn on the following sources:

Jugendbriefe von Robert Schumann, from originals provided by Clara Schumann (third edition. Leipzig, 1898).

Robert Schumann's Briefe, new series, edited by F. G. Jansen (second enlarged edition. Leipzig, 1904).

Jansen, *Die Davidsbündler* (Leipzig, 1883).

B. Litzmann, *Clara Schumann* (vols. i. and ii. Leipzig, 1903-1905).

BIOGRAPHICAL NOTE

ROBERT ALEXANDER, the youngest of the five children of Friedrich August Gottlob and Johanne Christiane Schumann, was born on June 8, 1810, at Zwickau, in Saxony. His father was a bookseller and something of an author. He took a keen interest in all literary and artistic matters, and encouraged similar tastes in his son. A great event in Robert's early life was a visit to Carlsbad, where he heard Moscheles. He was only nine years old, but the impression he received was so strong that he never lost the feeling of respect with which the great pianist inspired him. The only musical instruction he received at Zwickau was from Kuntzsch, the organist, who gave him pianoforte lessons for some years, and eventually announced that his pupil, for whom he prophesied a brilliant future, might safely dispense with tuition. Schumann's studies for pedal pianoforte, Op. 56, are dedicated to his old master. When he was fourteen he wrote some of the musical biographies in a work compiled by his father—a picture-gallery of famous men of every age and race. In 1826 his father died. Two years later Schumann left his quiet life at Zwickau, and went up to the University of Leipzig to study law, by his mother's wish. But he did not settle at Leipzig, and at Easter, 1829, removed to Heidelberg, attracted by the brilliant jurists attached to Heidelberg University, and also by the romantic associations of the place. His intention was to return to Leipzig after two years, and take his degree there; but although jurisprudence was presented in a more attractive light by Thibaut at Heidelberg, Schumann devoted more attention to philosophy and music than to his professional studies. He made little effort to master his antipathy to law, which he did not openly abandon, however, until the autumn of 1830, when he at length decided to adopt music as his profession. His mother considered music too precarious as a means of livelihood, and was only induced to consent to the change of plan when Schumann secured the support of Thibaut and Wieck. His acquaintance with Wieck (afterwards his father-in-law) dated from 1828, and he returned to Leipzig in October, 1830, to study pianoforte under him. But Wieck no longer taught him on the same methodical lines as during his earlier stay at Leipzig, and in the following autumn Schumann became anxious to change. He wrote to Hummel to offer himself as a pupil, but this plan was not carried out, and in 1832 he lamed the middle finger of his right hand permanently. He was therefore driven to turn his attention to composition and literary work. The winter of 1832-1833 was spent with his family at Zwickau and Schneeberg. Returning to Leipzig in the spring, he conceived the idea of starting, together with Wieck and others, a weekly musical paper (*Neue Zeitschrift für Musik*). The first number appeared on April 3, 1834, and was edited conjointly by Ludwig Schunke, Wieck, Julius Knorr, and Schumann. From 1835 to 1844 Schumann was sole editor. He was himself a large contributor, and mystified his public by an imaginary society, the *Davidsbund*. The original members of the *Davidsbund* were two, Florestan and Eusebius, fictitious personages evolved from Walt and Vult in Jean Paul Richter's *Flegeljahre*, who represented differing aspects of Schumann's own personality. Florestan stood for the masculine, energetic side of his temperament; Eusebius for its feminine, introspective tendencies. A third personage, Raro, represented a union of these two. Schumann's criticisms in the paper often took the form of imaginary conversations in which Florestan and Eusebius maintained opposite sides of the argument, Raro's judgment being invariably accepted as final. The further development of the *Davidsbund*, in which he incorporated many of his friends, is traced in Part III. of this book.

Schumann's attachment to Ernestine von Fricken, a pupil of Wieck's, led to an engagement; but he soon realized that he had mistaken his own feelings, and it was broken off in January, 1836, by mutual consent. He had set his heart on marrying

Wieck's daughter, Clara, the brilliant girl pianist, but Wieck persistently opposed a match which did not satisfy his ambitions for his daughter.[1] Schumann spent the winter of 1838-1839 in Vienna, where he hoped to establish himself with Clara, but he was unable to cope with the intrigues which surrounded him on all sides, and returned to Leipzig in the spring of 1839. On February 24, 1840, he received the honorary degree of Dr. Phil. from the University of Jena. In despair of obtaining Wieck's consent to their marriage, the lovers were finally driven to appeal to a court of law for permission, and were married at Schönefeld, a village near Leipzig, on September 12, 1840. A statement of the difficulties they had encountered is given by Schumann in a letter (No. 90) to the lawyer entrusted with the case.

In the spring of 1844 Schumann accompanied his wife to Russia on a concert tour. In October of the same year they left Leipzig, and by the doctor's advice went to live in Dresden. Schumann had been suffering from nervous depression, and it was hoped that he would gain some rest from music at Dresden, which was comparatively unimportant as a musical centre, In 1850 he accepted the post of conductor at Düsseldorf. This step seems to have been a fatal mistake. Schumann entirely failed as a conductor; his temperament was peculiarly unsuited to a public position of this sort, and the strain probably aggravated the mental disorder of

[1] See Introduction to Book II.

which he had shown signs even before his marriage. After the opening concert of the winter season in 1853 an attempt was made to lead him to resign, and from that time onwards both rehearsals and concerts were conducted by Tausch. An invitation to Schumann and his wife to give a number of concerts in Holland relieved them from the embarrassment of staying in Düsseldorf, and they started on their tour[1] in November, returning to Düsseldorf for Christmas. But Schumann's melancholy soon set in again, and in February, 1854, he attempted to take his life by throwing himself into the Rhine. He was removed to an asylum at Endenich, near Bonn, where he remained until his death on July 29, 1856.

Schumann's greatest activity as a composer dates from the time of his marriage. He produced, in rapid succession, songs, symphonies, chamber-music, and large dramatic works for chorus and orchestra. Most of his compositions are well known in this country. It was one of his cherished plans to visit England with his wife, but he never realized it. It was left to Madame Schumann to make the English public familiar with the beauties of her husband's pianoforte works after his death.

His power as a critic was very great. He was fearlessly outspoken and absolutely free from professional jealousy. If he erred, it was on the side of over-appreciation. His enthusiastic recogni-

[1] See Schumann's letter to his wife from Endenich, September 14, 1854.

tion of Chopin: 'Hats off, gentlemen; a genius!' is an instance of his attitude to new composers, and his last literary effort was a glowing article in the *Zeitschrift* which established Brahms's claim to be numbered in the first rank of composers at the very outset of his career. The breadth of his artistic sympathies is amply demonstrated in his letters.] [Tr.]

BOOK I

STURM UND DRANG

Weite Welt und breites Leben,
Langer Jahre redlich Streben,
Stets geforscht und stets gegründet,
Nie geschlossen, oft geründet,
Ältestes bewahrt mit Treue,
Freundlich aufgefaßtes Neue,
Heitern Sinn und reine Zwecke—
Nun—man kommt wohl eine Strecke!

Wolfgang Goethe.

(*Chosen as a motto by Schumann, in a letter to his mother of September* 21, 1831.)

'Thus it is ever in life. The aims we once pursued no longer satisfy us; we aim, we strive, we aspire, until sight fails, and mind and body find rest in the grave.'—*To his Mother, April 28, 1828.*

'There are strong souls on the borderland between genius and talent, who are equipped partly for action, partly for seeking the ideal. They are ambitious, intensely susceptible to the great and the beautiful—would give back their impressions to the world as their own creations; yet they succeed but imperfectly. Genius is one force tending to a centre of gravity, but these men are centres of gravity at which many forces meet and destroy one another. Thus they are poets, musicians, painters by turns. In youth they worship physical courage as the primary and direct expression of energy. Their delight in all great things comes from the hope of reproducing them, and it is turned to vexation of spirit when they fail. They ought to realize that it is they who have drawn the best prizes—if only they learn in time to curb their ambition—in that they possess varied and harmonious powers. They seem best fitted for full manhood by their enjoyment of the beautiful, in their moral completeness, and the wisdom of their thought. . . .'—*From* JEAN PAUL RICHTER'S *Titan* (quoted by Schumann in a letter of December 4, 1829, to his mother, as coincident 'to a hair's breadth' with his own case).

INTRODUCTION

EVEN Bohemianism is a vocation. In Schumann's case the ideas conjured up by the phrase 'artistic Bohemia' do not respond to the reality; the word Bohemian is, in fact, too foreign to describe him. On the other hand, he is the perfect type of the German romanticist, the very embodiment of the German romantic movement, if, indeed, man and artist are to be considered as an inseparable unity. Bohemianism, with its winged enthusiasms, was certainly compatible in his case—in spite of his scorn of the Philistines—with the utmost respectability. It accommodated itself to the 'cloistered virtue' so characteristic of Schumann, a virtue based on the practice of limitation as one of the arts of life, not on the narrow principles which guide the crowd.

Jean Paul thus formulated the rule of conduct which guided the German romanticists:

'I have never been able to discover more than

three ways of becoming, if not happy, at least happier. The first way of reaching the heights is to penetrate so far beyond the clouds of life that you see the wolves' dens, the charnel-houses and the lightning conductors far below you, diminished to the proportions of a miniature Dutch garden. The second is to fall right down into this garden, and there to nestle so cosily into a furrow that when you peer out of your warm lark's nest you see nothing of the dens, charnel-houses, and lightning conductors, but only the ears of corn, each of which forms a tree for the nesting-bird, a shelter from the sun and rain. Finally, the third, which I think both the hardest and the wisest, is to practise the two methods alternately.'

In this alternation, in fact, lies supreme wisdom. The alternation between the clouds and the nest in the narrow furrow was, indeed, the best result that our romanticists obtained. They generally began by trying to live their daily life in the cloudland which fostered their art. But life itself revolted against this misconception. The flight to the clouds resulted either in cowardly retreat from life or in that fundamentally barren and, moreover, hypocritical 'romantic irony' which gave way before the first attack.

The younger members of the group came in

time to agree with their senior, Jean Paul. They were driven to accept the theory of alternation if they desired happiness. It is not to be denied that in many cases a degree of success in the art of living was attained, the tranquil beauty of which sometimes inspires us men of to-day with a feeling of irrepressible envy. As a matter of fact envy is rarely justifiable with regard to individual romanticists. Their idea of alternation was to practise their art in cloudland, and to live their practical life in the furrow. For this reason the artistic production of the romanticists, especially their poetry, seems to us in most cases morbid or quite uninteresting, while the lives and intellectual development of the artists themselves strike us as being either contemptible or altogether unreal.

It is quite otherwise with the generation immediately following the romantic poets, with the painters and musicians of the romantic movement. Never since have the educated classes of Germany produced so many men of rare talent as in the years between the war of liberation and the revolution of 1848, the brilliant age of our classic writers, of the romanticists, and—he must have separate mention—Jean Paul. Instances of surpassing genius there were none. Flights into cloudland were, in art, kept within bounds, while the limits of life itself were considerably extended. Innumerable members of the learned and official classes were more than dilettanti in the modern sense. A study of the portraits of the time shows us how much harmony existed in individual cases. But such conditions easily breed complacent self-sufficiency, against which tendency the artists were again the first to struggle. 'Young Germany' was not alone in trying to uproot these conditions, for even to the essentially conservative Platen there was a false ring in the dictum, 'The morning for the law-courts; the evening for Helicon.'

There is, however, a third way, which differs from Jean Paul's solution. It lies, not in the alternation, but in the union of the two 'ways' indicated by him. Goethe has shown us how these two conflicting elements in German character can be blended to a harmonious whole. He is also a true classic, in that his life-work possesses enduring value when applied to entirely different conditions. He wrote and lived in the only way that ensures that harmonious plan of life which alone justifies the epithet 'happy.' That is to say, his feet were firmly placed on the solid, enduring earth; his forehead touched the stars. In Goethe's idea art not only provides high aims in life, but helps in the conduct of life by enabling us to turn our experience to practical use, and to achieve emancipation. Life not only appears valuable in itself, justifying its demand for men of action; but the artist who realizes life in its completeness only needs to come to closer quarters with humanity to find a rich field for his art.

These considerations on the nature of German romanticism are suggested by the study of Robert Schumann, because he was sensitive to the most varied influences. He was a true disciple of Jean Paul. Of all German musicians, or, we might almost say, of all German artists, none was so powerfully and permanently influenced by Jean Paul as Schumann, even though in later years his style did not betray its original model so clearly as in his youthful correspondence or in the early years of the *Zeitschrift*. This influence certainly was not confined to the form, but affected the innermost being of the man and the artist. He thought he had 'learnt more counterpoint from Jean Paul' than from any one of his music-teachers, and undoubtedly his moral outlook on life was derived from the same source, as his letters to his mother suffice to show. Evidently this kind, tender-hearted, beauty-loving, and impressionable woman was, like most German women, a devoted reader of the strangely fascinating poet. Schumann himself, as a young man, actually judged his fellows by their attitude towards Jean Paul.

The fact that Schumann was a typical example of the romantic double personality contributed largely to the close relations existing between the musician and the poet, though it is difficult to discriminate between cause and effect throughout. However much his original disposition may have contributed to the result, it is certain that his individual development in the direction of humorous melancholy—not melancholy humour—was encouraged by his all too early and too deep study of Jean Paul's writings.

Schumann's readiness to accept the theory of double personality, which was the dominating conception of his master's artistic activity, is most clearly shown by his adoption of a double ideal in his own intellectual life. The two individual tendencies figure in his writings as Florestan and Eusebius. The hand of Goethe can also be traced here, for Schumann always aimed at blending the two characters in the loftier unity to which he gave the name Raro. This acknowledged ideal was, however, rarely attained.

His dual nature emerges more clearly from a consideration of his personality as a whole. Titan's cloudy flights are there, side by side with the idyllic simplicity of dominie Wuz, and the problematic Walt and Vult of *Flegeljahre.* Schumann's activity as editor and his fiction of the *Davidsbündler* show this double-sidedness—childlike idealism bound up with a commercial genius in the management, not of his own affairs indeed, but of artistic matters generally. His ideas and his exertions for the organization of the musical profession, for concert arrangements, for the publication and printing of music (for instance, the note of the date of publication), have in many cases not yet been carried out, but are still desired by those who have the social improvement of the profession at heart.

There were thus quite opposite forces at work in Schumann, as is indeed the case with most men of genius. In the history of music the untroubled, harmonious development of Mozart is an isolated phenomenon. But when we think of the great romanticist Beethoven, whose life and art were almost always in opposition, like the double face of Janus, we soon realize what was lacking in Schumann. He also was Faust, but only Faust the seeker and idealist, consumed by his own desire; not Faust the man of action, to whom alone true happiness is revealed. Similarly the history of German romanticism contains many tragic conclusions following on fine beginnings, and the careers of the romanticists describe in nearly every case a descending curve after a splendid rise. Had the iron age of Napoleon exhausted the genius for action?

Nowhere are the 'limitations of humanity' more pronounced than in the practice of art, that most difficult of problems.

> 'Should he be lifted
> Up till he touches
> The stars with his forehead,
> Nowhere to rest find
> The insecure feet,
> And he is plaything
> Of clouds and of winds.
>
> 'Stands he with strong-knit
> Marrowy bone
> On the deep-seated,
> Enduring earth,
> No farther he reaches
> Than but with the oak
> Or the slenderer vine
> Himself to compare.'[1]

Even so, Schumann's flight led but to the dark, storm-driven clouds; his dreams ended in the impenetrable gloom of night.

But, at least, his end was sleep—tranquil melancholy—not the agony of terror. And it was

[1] Goethe's *Grenzen der Menschheit,* a translation by Captain William Gibson (*Poems of Goethe,* London, 1883).

preceded by a delightful flight into cloudland—a blissful dream of richly coloured fairy-pictures. As man and artist he remains worthy of the deepest affection. If his fate is a warning, his life has its lesson and its consolation in our own dull age.

PART I

1828-1840

JEAN PAUL AND DRYASDUST

'Jean Paul is still more to me than Schiller even; Goethe I do not yet understand.'—*To* FLECHSIG, *March* 17, 1828.

'All the world would be better for reading Jean Paul, if also unhappier. He has often brought me to the verge of madness, but through a mist of tears shines the rainbow of peace and a hovering spirit of humanity, and the heart is marvellously uplifted and gently illumined.'—*To* GISBERT ROSEN, *June* 5, 1828.

'Yet, believe me, were I ever to accomplish anything, it would be in music, which has always attracted me; and, without overestimating myself, I am conscious of possessing a certain creative faculty. But the study of jurisprudence, by which I must earn my bread, has so withered and frozen the flowers of my fancy that they will never again seek the light.'—*To his Mother, November* 11, 1829.

1.

To Flechsig[1] *at Leipzig.*

ZWICKAU, *March* 17, 1828.

. . . School days are over; the world lies before me. I could hardly keep back my tears as I came out of school for the last time, though I was really

[1] Emil Flechsig (1808-1878), a school friend of Schumann's, and a student of theology at Leipzig.

more glad than sorry. The time has come for me to show my mettle. Here I am, without guide, teacher, or father, flung helplessly into the darkness of life's unknown; and yet the world has never seemed fairer than at this moment, as I cheerfully face its storms. Flechsig, you must stand my friend in the whirl of life, and help me if I fall. Greek levity struck a happy mean between gay and grave in its outlook on life, and this is well enough in callow youth, but it must not degenerate into an unbalanced and inconsiderate frivolity. This is the time when a young man's soul glows with all things good and beautiful, and his ideals dwell with the gods of Greece in youth's bright Olympus. My friend, be my friend always, even should I prove unworthy of your friendship. Hold these lines before me as a warning, should I ever disgrace myself by not living up to what I have written here. . . .

2.

To his Mother[1] *at Zwickau.*

MONHEIM[2] NEAR NÜRNBERG, *April* 28, 1828.

. . . I often think of you, my dear good Mother, and of all the excellent maxims with which you

[1] Schumann's mother, Johanne Christiane Schnabel, born November 28, 1771, was the daughter of a surgeon at Zeitz. She married August Schumann in 1795. Robert was the youngest of their five children. She died February 4, 1836.

[2] Written during an expedition which Schumann made with his friend Rosen to Munich. They had taken this opportunity of making a pilgrimage to Jean Paul's home at Bayreuth.

armed me for the battle of life. . . . Dear Mother, how often have I offended you and misunderstood your wise intentions! Forgive your son, who hopes to atone for the faults of his hot-headed youth by good deeds and virtuous living. What a claim parents have on their child! Left fatherless, I have all the greater obligations towards you, dearest Mother. To you alone I owe my happy life, my prospect of a cheerful and cloudless future. May your child prove himself worthy, and respond ever and always to his Mother's love by leading a good life. But you must be, as always, my kind, forgiving Mother, and judge me leniently when I transgress, admonish me gently when my wildness plunges me too far into the dangerous labyrinth of life. Jean Paul says: 'Friendship and love traverse this globe closely veiled and with sealed lips, and no man speaks of his love to another, for the soul has no speech; but children's love may go unveiled, tell aloud its devotion to the parent's heart, and return adoration for love. . . .'

3.

To his Mother at Zwickau.

LEIPZIG, *May* 21, 1828.

Here is my first letter to you from Leipzig. Read, not only this one, but all my letters, beloved Mother, with the same kind, loving eyes, unclouded by anger.

I arrived here last Thursday, quite well, though a little depressed, and took my position as a student and a citizen in this big, spacious city, in the stir of life and the great world. After my few days here I still feel quite well, though not quite happy. My whole heart cries out for the quieter home where I was born and spent such happy days with Nature. How shall I come into touch with Nature here? Everything is distorted by art. There is neither valley, mountain, nor wood, where I can indulge in meditation, no spot where I can be alone, except this shut-up room, overlooking the noisy street. This is the bar to my satisfaction, besides which I am perplexed beyond measure by the choice of a study. Chilly jurisprudence, with its ice-cold definitions, would crush the life out of me from the start. Medicine I will not, theology I cannot study. Thus I struggle endlessly with myself, and look in vain for some one to tell me what to do. And yet—there is no help for it; I must choose law. However cut and dried it may be, I *will* conquer, and where there's a will there's a way. I shall also make a point of studying philosophy and history. Well, it will all come right. I will not look sadly into a future which may prove so happy if I stick to my purpose. . . .

4.

To his Mother at Zwickau.

LEIPZIG, *June* 13, 1828.

. . . As to my state of mind, it is neither worse nor better than before. I go regularly to lectures, practise two hours a day, read a few hours, or go for a walk—my sole recreation. At Zweinaundorf, a village lying in the loveliest part of the country round here, I often spend whole days alone, working, writing poetry, and so on. I have not cultivated the acquaintance of a single student so far. I go to the fencing-school, am sociable, and behave decently in every way, but am extremely cautious about becoming intimate with anyone. I find that, without being stand-offish, I can make these fellows keep their distance and not treat one as a freshman in the corps. Flechsig and Semmel[1] are the only two of whom I see much. In the law lectures I take notes mechanically, which is all I can do for the present. I should be very pleased if you would remember your kind promise about the riding-lessons.

5.

To his Mother.

LEIPZIG, *August* 3, 1828.

My best, best thanks, dearest Mother, for your pretty and elegant present. The students are all delighted with my magnificent stock, and admire your taste and your kind remembrances of your absent son. I often imagine myself back in the favourite old haunts at Carlsbad. What a happy child I was, and how little I realized it! Ah, why do we only appreciate our happiness when it is

[1] Moritz Semmel (1807-1874), brother of Schumann's sister-in-law Theresa. He studied law at Leipzig and Heidelberg, and became Geheimrat and magistrate at Gera.

past? Why does every tear that we shed symbolize a past joy or a vanished happiness? . . .

It is a great comfort to me to hear that you are feeling so well, in spite of your isolation and your quiet spiritual life. How well I can see you, as you take your solitary walks, gazing sadly up to the sky and longing to ask the Judge who sits in judgment above the stars, the Controller of our fates: 'Why hast Thou deprived me of those things which no life, no future, can restore?' Then, as you glance down, smiling, at the unfailing beauties of lavish Nature, your pious heart whispers, 'God knows best'; and as you look around you, more reconciled, you are able to say: 'Life is indeed beautiful, and man himself a tear of joy from the Godhead.' Ah, Mother! Nature best teaches how to pray, and how to reverence all the gifts the Almighty has given us. She is like a vast outspread handkerchief, embroidered with God's eternal name, on which we may dry alike our tears of sorrow and of joy; she turns weeping into ecstasy, and fills our hearts with speechless, quiet reverence and resignation. Why, in this hateful Leipzig, should every such higher enjoyment be denied? Why can I only attain the moments of my loftier happiness through sweet memories of what was once actual experience? But I have made my plans, and am only waiting to hear that you approve. As I must enter for my examination at Leipzig, and am bound to put in two years there, being a Saxon, I propose to go to Heidelberg next Easter, for the sake of hearing the most famous German jurists, Thibaut,[1] Mittermaier,[2] and others; I should return the following Easter, to get used to Leipzig methods again. My reasons for wishing to go to another university are three: first, on my own account, because I am not well here, and am getting extremely rusty: second, to gain knowledge of the world; and third, for the sake of my profession, because the most famous jurists are at Heidelberg. If I go at all, it must certainly be next Easter; going later would mean taking my examination immediately on my return. I should then do very badly in Saxon law, and thus disappoint both you and myself. They examine chiefly in that subject here, and I should certainly have forgotten it in the meantime, as I have to take Roman law, the Pandects, etc., at Heidelberg. Please write and tell me what you think. We can *talk* it over later, as I am to spend the whole of the Michaelmas and Christmas vacations at Zwickau.

[1] Anton Friedrich J. Thibaut (1772-1840), a famous lecturer on law at Heidelberg, rendered an important service by awakening interest in old music. He wrote on this subject in his still readable book, *Über Reinheit der Tonkunst* (1824).

[2] K. J. A. Mittermaier (1787-1867) occupied the chair of Penal Law at Heidelberg.

6.

To G. Rosen.[1]

LEIPZIG, *August* 14, 1828.

It must be a confoundedly queer pleasure to read my Sanskrit. I really will write quite beautifully to-day, and make a rule of the exception, the rule being that poets and pianists all write a terrible fist, of which mine is typical. The *captatio benevolentiæ* is over; here begins the real letter.

Oh, the good old times, when you were 'Baron' Rosen, *malgré vous!* Your descent from the baronial elevation marked the beginning of my noble career—in other words, my college days. But what a barren waste it is, with neither 'roses' nor 'Rosen'! I indulge in a flight with Jean Paul or at the piano occasionally, thereby scandalizing these good Germans and Jahnians.[2] The Icaruses and aeronauts of the imagination are to the stick-in-the-muds and scavengers as bees to human beings. On the wing they harm no one; but try to touch them on a flower, and they sting. If I have not actually stung anyone, I kicked and struggled, hoping to send these intangible con-

[1] Gisbert Rosen (1808-1876), of Göttingen, a school friend of Schumann's, became chief magistrate of Detmold.

[2] F. L. Jahn was the founder of gymnastic schools the primary object of which was the encouragement of the military spirit. [Tr.]

ceptions of people's rights, nationality, etc., to the right-about. Götte[1] is one of those strong characters who are now so rare; he detests all poisonous lyricism and sentimentality, and combines heroism with common sense. I see him daily; he is my only intimate acquaintance. None of the others interest me particularly. I might, perhaps, make friends with Schütz and Günther, were they less narrow-minded. There is talk of suspending the constitution—a very good thing, I should say; the lesser lights would be snuffed and then extinguished, and the greater trimmed and brightened. Semmel has withdrawn into his shell, and only indulges in occasional tirades, creating many enemies, whom he treats with the scorn they deserve.

I am certainly coming to Heidelberg, but not until Easter, 1829, worse luck! If only you were still there, to enjoy that paradise with me! Many thanks for the charming little pictures, which lent wings to my dreams, and transported me instantly to my home by the Neckar. I have not been to a single lecture yet, but have been working at home—that is, played the piano and written a few letters and *Jean-Pauliades*. I have not much faith in you as a voluminous correspondent either, but don't forget any of your real friends—I mean myself.

I am not intimate with any families yet. Indeed, I avoid my deplorable kind, I hardly know why, and very seldom go out. The puerilities of this

[1] Wilhelm Götte, of Brunswick, studied philology at Leipzig

selfish world appal me. Imagine a world without inhabitants: one vast cemetery, the dreamless sleep of death, Nature with no flowers, no spring, a broken peepshow without figures; and yet, what is this inhabited world of ours? The same: God's acre of buried dreams, the sleep of death troubled with visions of blood, a garden of cypress and weeping willow, a silent peepshow with sorrowing figures. Such it is, God knows!

Whether we shall meet again, the fates alone can tell, but the world is not big enough, after all, to keep people apart, particularly real friends. Let us not bewail our losses, for fate has always sealed the mouths of men with her giant hand, though never their hearts. Love grows more intense, and esteem more sacred, through separation, because intercourse with an invisible friend is tinged with the spiritual or supernatural. . . .

And now, farewell, Rosen. May your life have no more clouds than go to a beautiful sunset, no more rain than makes the moon-rainbow that you see from the castle ruins, as you look over the fair valley in the starlight. Above all, don't forget your distant friend, who is so sore and unhappy, and wish me all the things I wish you from afar. Let your gentle, humane spirit soar lightly above the mire, and be ever as you now are, and ever were, the most humane of men. . . .

Farewell!

Your

SCHUMANN.

7.

To his Mother.

HEIDELBERG, *May* 24, 1829.

Take up your spectacles, my beloved Mother, for postage is dear now, and I must write very, very small. You will gather from my tone that I am not unhappy. Indeed, no one could be unhappy in my princely room, facing the glorious old castle and the green oak forests, without sinning unpardonably against his own soul. I think you will not be bored by extracts from my pocket-book about my little journey.

The way from Leipzig to Frankfurt was like a perpetual flight through spring skies, and a constant succession of pleasant and lively travelling companions made up to some extent for the unavoidable fatigue of the night journey. I soon made friends with Willibald Alexis,[1] and we were inseparable until he branched off to the north, I to the south. There was a curious mail-coach passenger, named R——, a Prussian secretary of embassy, on his way to the Federal Diet at Frankfurt. I had hardly exchanged two words with him when he began to describe *ex abrupto* the perfections of his wife in Berlin, assuring me that his whole life and happiness were bound up with her. He recited poems in her praise, and showed me her portrait in miniature. I confess it was my first experience

[1] The well-known historical novelist (1798-1871), whose real name was Häring.

of the sort, but I liked him, for he was evidently good and intelligent. Alexis amused himself by putting him into his new novel there and then. My other travelling companions were a Frankfurt Jew trader, whose conversation was of leather and other dull matters; a worthy old lady who was full of the Gotha theatre; and two French Jews who drank an uncommon deal of wine, and talked nonsense all night. Please admire my wonderful gift of observation, as displayed in this description!

But now comes a change in the journey. We had barely arrived at Hanau when we turned round a corner to the right, towards Frankfurt. The whole sky changed with us, and became clear, blue and unclouded—like my eyes at this moment—maintaining this benevolent attitude the whole way. We were, indeed, in a new key. The lovely Main lay at our feet, with craft of all sizes on its mirror-like surface, and accompanied us with its chattering as far as Frankfurt. All the trees were laden with blossom, the high corn waved in the breeze, with yellow charlock springing amongst it. The birds flew up, singing, from the fields, to welcome me to Frankfurt. But I cannot tell you all about Frankfurt to-day, or this letter would be the size of a folio volume. . . .

I described a sentimental journey yesterday, but will now tell you of the interesting sights and antiquities I saw on the 14th. I was seized, first thing, by an irresistible desire to play the piano. So I walked coolly into the first piano-shop, represented myself as the tutor of a young English lord, commissioned to buy a grand piano, and played for three whole hours, astonishing and delighting the natives. I promised to give them the supposed lord's decision in two days, but by that time I was safe in Rüdesheim, drinking Rüdesheimer. I love to explore the out-of-the-way nooks and alleys of old towns, and as Alexis has the same fad, we spent four hours in the quaintest parts of the city. How dull our modern architecture is, with its symmetrical streets, two miles long, compared to a place like this, where every turn brings something new and interesting!

Legationsrat Georg Düring had invited us to his house in the afternoon, where we saw his clever wife and Mrs. Ferdinand Ries,[1] a perfectly lovely Englishwoman. Her English was like an angel's lisping. We talked French mostly, and as I quite outshone Alexis I felt grateful for once to Bodmer.[2] We then went with Düring to the Städel Museum, Goethe's house, and Bethmann's garden. Dannecker's Ariadne! Imagine the highest and loveliest type of womanhood, in the full pride of serene beauty, and a foaming panther, obedient to the touch of her light, triumphant fingers. Her steed, for all his restiveness, nuzzles her hand, and her

[1] Wife of Ferdinand Ries (1784-1838), Beethoven's pupil, who had lived twelve years in England and married there. Schumann's strong partiality for Englishwomen found expression in a letter to his mother on September 27, 1830: 'If ever I marry, it will be an Englishwoman.'

[2] Schumann's teacher at Zwickau.

head is proudly uplifted. Is it not a sublime picture of beauty's power to bind all things, even brute strength, with a spell? The marble is milky-blue, of the finest Carrara. It stands in a room shaded with many-coloured hangings. Through one of these, of burning red, the sun came, and the marble shone like transparent snow flushed by the dawn. But no more! Such things are beyond description. . . .

On Saturday we looked round Wiesbaden. A letter of introduction from Rohde, the secretary of embassy, proved very useful. Wiesbaden is prettily situated, but its marble palaces and buildings bore me by their sameness. I really hate all these avenues, castles, and parks, and infinitely prefer the unpretentious streets and houses of Frankfurt and Nürnberg. We left Wiesbaden at nine. I had closed my eyes just before coming in sight of our majestic old Father Rhine, so as to enjoy to the full my first glimpse of his unruffled waters. There he lay, serene and proud as an old German god, surrounded by a paradise of mountain, valley, and glorious vineyard. Within six hours we passed through Hochheim, Erbach, Hattenheim, Marcobrunnen, Geisenheim, etc. . . .

We arrived at Rüdesheim at five. After some refreshment, both liquid and solid, we started from Assmannshausen for the Niederwald, for the sake of the finest view in the whole bewitching Rhine scenery. As for the old Rhine castles, the wonders of one's youth, it is the same with them as with everything else. The first sends you into raptures, and you think you must climb up to every one, but the novelty soon wears off. The fine ruin of Ehrenfels was the first I saw, and it looked down proudly enough on me and on the Mouse Tower in the Rhine. You know the legend. There was a majestic sunset, and the dusk crept up slowly. On the Rüdesheim shore boats, astir with life, were swinging at anchor; old gaffers sat smoking their pipes outside the houses, and children playing on the banks made such a picture that we nearly missed the moonrise. The calm became deeper and deeper. I ordered a glass of Rüdesheimer. An old boatman and his little girl took me on to their boat. There was not a ripple; the sky was blue and clear, and the moonlit waters magically reflected Rüdesheim with its dark Roman ruins. Above it all, on a high peak, stood the lovely Rochus Kapelle. I was filled with emotion as we rowed backwards and forwards. The fisherman's Pomeranian lay at his master's feet, wagging his tail, and I called his name to hear it echo. 'Anchor! Anchor! Anchor!' came back to me from the hills. Then I called 'Robert.' We landed, and in the silver moonlight the flowing tide lulled the wanderer to sleep. . . .

On Wednesday, May 20, I went gaily on board the steamer *Friedrich Wilhelm* at 6 a.m. sharp. The company was fairly select; but I took refuge from the commonplace chatter with some veteran Dutch soldiers in the third class, and made them tell me of battles, particularly of Waterloo. The appointments of the steamer are truly princely, but the hubbub on deck amused me more than anything. I wish I could have sketched some of the groups: two old warriors sleeping on their knapsacks in a corner; two very fine students pacing up and down; two ladies in fits of laughter; sailors in red shirts stoking the furnace; a spectacled artist making lightning sketches; an Englishman grimacing furiously as he pulls his choker over his ears; a white-capped cook carrying raw steaks, and so busy that he hardly knows where to turn; and myself as I sit writing poems and taking in everything at the same time. And see! the obsequious steward dashes in my direction with a glass of Rüdesheimer, etc. The saloons are splendidly furnished with silk-covered divans, mahogany and bronze fittings, red silk curtains, large window-like mirrors, and are perfectly arranged in every way. Excellent table d'hôte, the best wines, all the papers, chess, billiards even—for there was so little vibration below that the balls lay quite motionless—everything, in a word, that body and soul could require. Need I say more? Yet I longed to be on deck again. The whole afternoon I sat alone, bareheaded, right in the bows, drank coffee, smoked some good cigars given me by an Englishman, thoroughly enjoyed the tearing wind in my hair, and even composed an ode to the north-east wind which really isn't half bad.

They all thought me very eccentric, and one of

the crew said I should make a splendid sailor, because I could face the blast bareheaded.

We could see Mainz, with its glorious red towers and its array of boats, gleaming through the trees. We arrived at 7 p.m., and, for the first time in the whole journey, I made a most wretched meal, at the Three Imperial Crowns. Then I pottered about the streets and churches. At night I went over my accounts, and was not altogether surprised to find that I had literally only three florins left to count. So, when I went to bed, my meditations were not altogether pleasant.

Next morning, May 21, I went for a drive in a wretched hired conveyance with a jovial major who might have walked out of Clauren,[1] moustache and all. He had been aide-de-camp to Murat in Naples and Spain, and had been condemned to death with him, but subsequently acquitted. Naturally, I let him do the talking. I did not see one pretty face between Mainz and Heidelberg. At Worms we lunched, then saw the Cathedral and the Lutheran Church, in which Luther made his confession of faith. We asked the guide how old the church was. 'A hundred and twenty years,' was the answer. We laughed, but my laugh was none of the lightest when I happened to touch my waistcoat pocket! The gallant major left me, unfortunately, before Mannheim, which I reached about 4 o'clock. Driving was out of the question, for obvious reasons; but I was quite content

[1] A sensational novelist of the period. [Tr.]

to walk, as I saw prospects of a stormy evening and a gorgeous sunset. So I did not stay in Mannheim, you see. On the way I passed the very signpost where Sand is standing, lost in thought, in the picture that hangs in our drawing-room. There was a splendid sky, and the sun went down majestically in a blaze of purple. About 9 o'clock I reached my dear Heidelberg with strangely mingled emotions.

And now, my dearest Mother, I will put this small, but very pleasant picture of a fragment of my life's journey in its frame, and close. You may expect in my next letter a detailed description of life in Heidelberg, to which my good friend Rosen is to introduce me. You will read this letter as I write it, in the spirit of affection.

Your

ROBERT.

8.

To his Mother.

HEIDELBERG, *July* 17, 1829.

. . . It is some consolation to hear that Julius[1] is a little better. In every letter I open I shall hope

[1] Julius, Schumann's youngest brother, died in 1833. Schumann always kept up a close intercourse with his brothers and sisters and relations, and was on the most affectionate terms with his sisters-in-law. The family consisted of: 1. Eduard (1797-1839), who married Theresa Semmel (1803-1887) of Gera. Theresa afterwards married the bookseller Fleischer, of Leipzig. 2. Karl (1801-1849), who married (1) Rosalie Illing (1808-1833), and (2) Pauline Colditz (1818-1879). 3. Julius (1805-1833), who married Emilia Lorenz (1810-1860). 4. Emilia (1807-

to find an advance towards 'quite well.' We are relatively more cast down by failure than uplifted by success, and our appreciation of health varies according to the amount of it we possess—inversely. As for me, I am in excellent spirits, really happy by moments, and am working well and steadily. Thibaut and Mittermaier have given me a taste for law. I begin to realize its true value in furthering the highest interests of mankind. And oh! the difference between that Leipzig automaton, with one eye on a regular professorship, reading out his dull paragraphs phlegmatically, and Thibaut here, who, though twice his age, overflows with vivacity and intelligence, and can hardly find time or words to express all his ideas. Everything here is on a smaller scale than in Leipzig, more provincial and less varied; but I like it, though I often miss the many-sided interest of a large town. It is hard to say which is better for the student. The Heidelberg student is much misrepresented. He is very quiet, rather apt to stand upon ceremony and affect fine manners, because he is not yet sure of himself. His importance in the town and neighbourhood is unquestioned, and it is not surprising that the natives show him exaggerated civility, for he makes the place. But I think it is a pity for a young man to come

1826), who drowned herself in an attack of fever. With the exception of this incident, there were no symptoms of mental disease in Robert's family, but none of his brothers and sisters lived to old age.

to a town where the student holds undisputed sway. A young man of any grit develops best under a system of repression, and this perpetual lounging with no one but students limits his mental outlook, and injures him incalculably for practical life. From this point of view large towns are preferable, and Leipzig is better than Heidelberg. Fortunately, I am sufficiently sobered to value things at their proper worth. I should certainly let any son of mine study one year at Heidelberg and three at Leipzig. But Heidelberg has always this advantage, that its fine scenery does much to distract students from dissipation and drinking. They are far steadier here than at Leipzig.

And yet, my gay Heidelberg, what sweet innocence, what idyllic charm is yours! If the Rhine with its mountains be a type of manly beauty, the Neckar may stand for female loveliness—the one massive and severe as old Teutonic harmonies, the other gentle as the melodies of Provence. The accompanying views will enable you to picture me in my favourite haunts, where I sit and dream of nothing, or of Zwickau and you, Julius, Eduard, and every one. . . .

Music here is at a very low level. There is not a decent pianist in the place. My own playing is considered quite exceptional. I have not found my way into any families yet. Time enough for that in the winter, when I shall no doubt be glad to go out a good deal, as there are plenty of girls here to make love to! You meet dozens of students engaged—with the consent of the parents. The girls naturally lose their sentimental hearts to the only men they see, and, as they meet no one but students, engagements among them are the order of the day. But have no fear for me; my very frankness should disarm you. I have been neglecting my piano badly, but hope to make up for it in the winter. Summer for play, winter for work! . . .

9.

To his Mother.

HEIDELBERG, *August* 3, 1829.

MY DEAR, DEARLY-LOVED MOTHER,

Your letter, which was brought to me a moment ago in bed, roused me effectually from my slumbers and dreams. I read and read, and could hardly believe it came from you, until I realized the motherly tenderness which prompted it all. The whole story is this: The holiday is none of my making, but the usual Michaelmas vacation, which is purposely fixed early by the Senate, so that students may see something of Switzerland and Northern Italy. At Leipzig they give six weeks, here eight; so, you see, I don't miss a single lecture. You will by this have had another letter giving full explanations. I have been doing French and Italian with Semmel, and speak both fairly well; but this trip would enable me to perfect myself in both languages, and would be infinitely cheaper and more satisfactory than a whole year's lessons. Besides, no student spends the vacation at Heidelberg. Switzerland is only twenty hours distant, and Italy not much farther. Think how many of the Leipzig students contrive to go without missing any lectures, and here am I, five times as near, with two months to spare—how could I help going? Who could resist such names as these: Domo d'Ossola, Arona, Lago Maggiore, Milano, Brescia, Verona, Padua, Venezia? I am sure you will forgive me, and say: 'My dear Robert, a young man like yourself must travel, and clip his clumsy wings a little, so that he may learn to soar more lightly. True, it is expensive, but you will see a new world and new people; you will learn French and Italian, and, in fact, great results justify some outlay' etc. . . .

Write again, if you can, my dearest Mother—another good, inspired letter like the last—and I should not object to a few ducats towards my travelling expenses! Heaven and Eduard[1] permitting, my next letter will be from Milan. You will receive whole volumes about my journey, which will amuse you in the long, dull winter evenings. . . .

10.

To his Mother.

BERNE, *August* 31, 1829.

. . . You will have had my letter from Basle. If the world seemed a paradise then, I am now in

[1] Eduard was to provide the money. [Tr.]

the ninety-ninth heaven. The poet sees better than other mortals. I do not see things as they are, but according to my own subjective impression, and this makes life easier and simpler. For the last few days, for instance, the weather has been vile, the Alps and glaciers all hidden by lowering clouds; but the world only looms the more vividly in the imagination for being partially obscured, and I very likely pictured the shadowy Alps finer than they really are. Then, you may say, why not stay at home with your nose in a book, and leave the Alps to their own devices? But I should argue in return that there is a charm in being so far away and in the presence of classic mountains, which awakens a hundred precious emotions, not to speak of the practical advantages of travel.

After this somewhat learned dissertation I will continue my letter from Basle in Hogarthian, Titianesque touches! The Englishmen on the coach rather wondered at my choosing the uncomfortable box-seat, as the morning air was fresh. But you will understand when I tell you that I was able, from my perch, to make flying remarks to a young widow from Havre de Grace sitting inside, who responded with glances that were anything but mournful. You see, I tell you all my little weaknesses. I can give you no idea of the fertility and beauty of the pastures and meadows. We drove along the banks of the Rhine. On the other side rose the young Alps in their green beauty, which makes them as bright, sturdy children compared with the grand gray Alps which look down benignly on us here. I spent the night at Baden (not Baden-Baden), a gay little *Bad*, and for once I met a good many Germans. There was music, and, of course, we danced, the mournful widow displaying as much sprightliness as if her husband had been living. . . . From Zurich I walked over the Albis to Zug. I should like you to read these letters map in hand, and so follow me in imagination. It was a glorious ramble, and not tiring, thanks to the constantly varying scenery. I tramped along in solitude, my knapsack on my 'hump,' swinging my alpenstock in the Alpine air, and stopping every few minutes to drink in some fresh aspect of this Swiss paradise. We are not, after all, quite unhappy, if our hearts respond to the touch of Nature. I skipped down the Albis like a gazelle; but the view of those wooded, ice-capped peaks with flocks on the slopes, the lakes, spreading like peacocks, and the sound of village chimes and tinkling cow-bells from the heights, sobered me, and I walked slowly on with my eyes riveted on the mountains.

Spare me to-day the description of my first climb on the Rigi, when I found myself at a vast height above the everyday world, and watched the sun set and rise again. Absolute strangers mixed together like members of one family—I even soon succeeded in drawing pretty glances from a pretty Englishwoman!—and Switzerland lay before me in her primeval grandeur. . . .

Distance, which dulls the visual world, only renders the world of memory more distinct. Enthusiasm is changed to glowing classic calm, and its expression is refined to a Goethe-like thoughtfulness. So tremble for the description to come, the labyrinth of words to be struggled through. To-morrow I leave for Lake Maggiore, by way of the Gemmi pass, and hope to reach Milan in five or six days.

11.

To his Sister-in-law, Theresa Schumann.

BRESCIA, *September* 16, 1829.

I have just been reminded of you by a beautiful Italian woman, and thus it occurred to me to write, my dear Theresa. I wish I could give you a picture of it all: the deep blue skies of Italy; the luxuriant grass springing at my feet; groves of apricot and lemon trees, of flax, silk, and tobacco; the flowery carpet; the soft southern air astir with butterflies; the distant, immovable Austrian Alps, sinewy and jagged; the fine, flashing eyes of the Italian women, much like yours when you are enthusiastic about anything; the whole intoxicating and spontaneous movement of life; the poetry of the place, which almost makes me forget even the beloved Germany to which my whole nature clings; and my truly German sentimental fashion of gazing around me at the abundant foliage, or at the setting sun, or at the Alps as they glow red under the sun's parting kiss, and then become cold, monstrous, and lifeless. If I could depict all this for you, I should run to such volumes that you would have to pay double postage. . . .

It was lovely weather yesterday when I left Milan, where I had loitered for six days, having meant to stay only two. I had many reasons for staying: first, the best possible, that I really liked it; second, the particular attractions, such as the cathedral, the Palazzo reale, the *escalier conduisant du Belvedere* in the Reichmann Hotel, and a beautiful Englishwoman, who seemed to have fallen in love, less with me than my piano-playing. Englishwomen are all like that; they love with their intellects—that is, they love a Brutus, a Lord Byron, a Mozart, or a Raphael, and are not so much attracted by the physical beauty of an Apollo or an Adonis, unless it enshrines a beautiful mind. Italian women do the exact opposite, and love with their hearts only. German women love with both heart and intellect as a rule, unless they fall in love with a circus-rider, a dancer, or some Crœsus ready to marry them on the spot. All this quite impersonally and *sans comparaison*, please. The third inducement to stay is offered by a certain Graf S., of Innsbruck, with whom I found I had intellectually much in common, despite the fact that he is fourteen years older than I. We found a great deal to tell each other, and joked and gossiped a great deal, to our mutual satisfaction, as it seemed. He was a living proof that the world is not composed of boors and apes, for all that he was rather deaf, stooped badly, and made terrible grimaces, not so much at the world generally as at individuals.

I should not hear a note of decent music here, were not the whole Italian language in itself perpetual music. Graf S. calls it a long-sustained chord in A minor. . . . My Italian really serves me very well, but it is practically the rule in Italy to fleece foreigners. I pose as a Prussian, because Prussians have the best name here. It is a useful and perfectly harmless wrinkle, though it is sad to have to deny one's fatherland.

12.

To his Sister-in-law, Rosalie Schumann, at Schneeberg.

MILAN, *October* 5, 1829.

We are indeed the playthings of Fate, Rosalie. I wanted to be, and ought to have been, at Innsbruck a week ago, yet here I am, stuck fast in Milan for the second time. I shall find it impossible to write much to-day, having small desire to bore you and myself. Here, then, is my tale of woe, short and to the point, in seven chapters, beginning with my state of health in Venice, and ending to-day. You will, I hope, have received my letter to Emilia from there.

Here goes, then:

Chapter I.—A beautiful evening tempted me on to the water; I took a gondola, and floated far, far out. Heaven knows, I am quite at home in a boat, and yet I turned sea-sick on the way back.

Chapter II.—Pains, aches, spasms, headache, diarrhœa, and nausea—a death in life.

Chapter III.—In my fright I put myself in the hands of a doctor, who really cured me as quickly as I could have done it myself—in three days; but he demanded a napoleon for his trouble, which I was kind enough to pay him.

Chapter IV.—After a careful search in my purse, it turned out to be impossible in this case (although, according to my favourite system, everything is possible) to get back to Germany. Consequent change of plans (see Chapter VI.).

Chapter V.—On the top of these financial and other difficulties, I was the victim of a scandalous theft. A merchant with whom I had travelled from Brescia absconded with a napoleon of mine, leaving me barely enough to pay for my lodging in Venice.

Chapter VI.—Tragic struggle between good and evil. Should I or should I not sell the watch my mother gave me? Virtue won the day, and I decided I would far rather undertake the thirty miles journey.

Chapter VII. (the last).—Finds me squeezed up in a corner of the coach, pondering with sad and stolid countenance the enviable fate of those students who are sitting snugly with their sisters-in-law. I was cursed, in fact, with a violent attack of home-sickness. Then I had a pretty vision of

Zwickau at sunset, when folk sit out on their benches, and children play or paddle in the rippling streams, just as I once did, and much besides. . . .

These, my dear Rosalie, are the joys of travelling in Italy. You will easily believe how good it was to hear German again at the Reichmann Hotel in Milan. My first request in that town was for money. I went to Reichmann, who had offered to lend me some on my first visit, and he gave me sixteen napoleons on the spot, without inquiring into my circumstances or those of my family, and without charging any interest. A German of the right sort!

So here, dear people, you have, packed into one page, an account of all my woes, from the like of which Heaven deliver you. But don't be in the least worried about your depressed kinsman, even though he has to climb many awful mountains before seeing Germany again.

13.

To Friedrich Wieck.[1]

HEIDELBERG, *November* 6, 1829.

I have but just laid aside Hummel's concerto in A minor, my dear Master. It was the work of a moment to pull down my blind, light my cigar, pull

[1] Friedrich Wieck (1785-1873) was one of the most famous German teachers of the pianoforte. Schumann had made his acquaintance shortly after his arrival in Leipzig, and himself reaped great advantage from the instruction given by Wieck to Clara. He could not then bring himself to regular study, and especially detested theory, which he considered superfluous. (*Cf.* the introduction to Part II.)

up the table, and bury my face in my hand, and in a flash I was transported to the corner of the Reichsstrasse,[1] my music under my arm ready for my piano lesson. Ah! what possessed me to leave Leipzig? There I had access to the Olympus of music, and you, its priest, at hand to lift the veil with gentle decision from the eyes of the dazzled novice. Here it is very much as I expected. There is on the whole a great love for music, but little talent. Here and there an antiquated critic or two, but little creative power. As you know, I have small taste for crude theory, and have been going my own way quietly, improvising a good deal, but playing very little from notes. I have begun several symphonies, but have finished nothing. Now and again I squeeze in a Schubert valse between Roman law and the Pandects, and the trio haunts my dreams, bringing back the heavenly hour when I first heard it at your house. I think I may say I have not lost much ground, neither have I made any appreciable progress—practically a standstill, I admit. Still, I feel that my touch is much fuller in *forte*, more supple and responsive in *piano*, although I may have lost in fluency and precision. Without undue vanity, I cannot help feeling modestly conscious of my superiority over all the other Heidelberg pianists. . . .

I am now working up the last movement of Hummel's F sharp minor sonata. It is truly a titanic work, epic in character, describing the

[1] Wieck's house at Leipzig.

mighty struggles of a giant mind and its eventual resignation. I shall play you only this at Easter, so you may make it a test of my progress.

There is a strong party, in which I figure, now forming against Thibaut.[1] You would hardly believe what delightful, refreshing hours I have spent with him, and yet how his one-sided and really pedantic views on music grieve me, knowing, as I do, his broad-mindedness in jurisprudence, and the irresistible power of his brilliant, dominating intellect.

I returned from my tour in Switzerland and Italy a fortnight ago, poorer by a few napoleons, but richer by my increased knowledge of the world and a store of precious memories. I declare you can have no notion of Italian music until you have heard it under the Italian skies which called it into being. How often did I think of you in the Scala Theatre at Milan! How charmed I was with Rossini, or rather with Pasta's[2] interpretation. I leave her name unqualified to show my respect—I might say, my adoration. In the Leipzig concert-room I sometimes experienced a thrill of awe in the presence of the genius of music, but Italy has taught me to love it. Only once in my whole life have I had an impression of the actual presence of God, of gazing reverently and unrebuked into His face; this was at Milan, as I listened to Pasta—

[1] See, however, letter 14. [Tr.]

[2] Italian opera should, indeed, never be judged by German representations. Pasta (1798-1865) not only sang, but acted brilliantly, especially in passionate parts.

and Rossini! Do not smile, dear Master, for I speak seriously. But this was my sole musical treat in Italy. Their music is, in the ordinary way, hardly fit to listen to. You have no conception of the sort of slapdash facility with which they reel off everything. . . .

Schubert[1] is still my 'one and only' love, the more so as he has everything in common with my one and only Jean Paul. To play his compositions is with me like reading one of Jean Paul's novels. . . . There is no other music which presents so bewildering a psychological problem in its train of ideas, its apparently abrupt transitions. It is rare to find a composer who can stamp his individuality plainly on such a heterogeneous collection of tone-pictures, and still rarer are those who write, as Schubert did, as their hearts prompt them. Schubert unburdened his heart on a sheet of music-paper, just as others leave the impression of passing moods in their journals. His soul was so steeped in music that he wrote notes where others use words—so, at least, I venture to think. Some years back I began a book on the æsthetics of sound, and made some way with it; but I soon realized that I had neither enough ripe judgment nor a sufficiently objective attitude, consequently sometimes finding what others had missed and *vice versa.* But if you only knew my perpetual state of ferment! Why, I might have arrived at Op. 100

[1] Schumann was the first to recognize Schubert's full greatness, and did much to induce a juster estimate of his work.

with my symphonies, had I written them out. I feel so entirely in my element with a full orchestra; even if my mortal enemies were marshalled before me, I could lead them, master them, surround them, or repulse them. Circumstances rather than principles keep me from undue presumption, though I occasionally take a high tone with people who provoke it. But there are times when my soul so overflows with melody that it is impossible to write anything down; at such times I could laugh in the face of any art critic who should tell me that I had better write nothing, since I cannot excel, and boldly say he knew nothing about it. Forgive these wonderful revelations. And now for the favours I have to ask. The first and most pressing is—write to me; the second—very soon. Your letters mean positively as much to me here as the Leipzig concerts I have to miss. So you have had Paganini[1] at Leipzig, and heard him four times! Really, that *four* is too tantalizing. . . .

14.

To his Mother.

HEIDELBERG, *February* 24, 1830.

. . . Thibaut is really divine; my happiest hours are those I spend with him. Every Thursday a chorus of over seventy meets at his house to practise one of Händel's oratorios. He accom-

[1] Schumann had heard Paganini at Frankfurt, and the fascination of his playing undoubtedly strengthened his own desire to become a virtuoso.

panies at the piano himself like one inspired. When it is over I see the tears come into those fine eyes of his, overshadowed by his silvery hair, and, when he comes up to me, grasping my hand speechless with delight, I wonder how a poor beggar like myself comes to be honoured with an invitation to a house where I can hear such glorious music. You can have no idea of his wit, his acuteness of perception, his real feeling for art, his kindness, his tremendous eloquence, and unfailing tact. . . .

You may judge from this, my dear Mother, that my stay in Heidelberg is pleasant, inspiring, gay and varied—adjectives that would have to be put in the superlative degree should I stay longer. This brings me to the reason of my long and timorous silence. Julius wrote to me, too, saying: 'You must on no account think of coming at Easter. Stay at Heidelberg till Michaelmas, at least. It is hardly worth while to make so considerable a journey for the sake of those few months' lectures. Think it over very carefully, for, once away, you may find it not so easy to return. Besides, you can undoubtedly pursue your law studies more profitably and pleasantly at Heidelberg than at Leipzig, which is so badly off for jurists.' So says dear old Julius. Please give him a brotherly greeting from me for the whole of his affectionate letter; another to Emilia for her piquant French epistle. And now, in the fewest possible words, to my request and my carefully considered reasons. Shall you be angry if I extend my term of absence from a year to eighteen months? Please let me have your answer as soon as possible, for I have been secretly counting on your consent for a month past. Also, in the case of my return to Zwickau, I should have very little time left, and much, very much, to do in the way of preparation and settling up accounts. The only argument against a longer stay in Heidelberg is the everlasting, tiresome question of money. Indeed, it would cost me just as much again. And yet I am in the flush of youth, not quite poverty-stricken, with the prospect of many precious moments here. I have some splendid friends, fine fellows in themselves, and shall I really disturb all this and wreck my hopes for the sake of 200 florins?

I speak as seriously as the matter deserves. If you have any proposals, dear Mother, do make them, and they are sure to meet with my acceptance. However great my longing to see you all may be, who knows whether a longer separation might not rather heighten and purify it? The truest love lies more in the spirit and in the imagination than in externals. The best way of learning to love is to be sent away for ten years among strangers; the result is a strong, undimmed affection. So do please write, dear Mother, or send me a word of loving consent—a ring to wed me to Heidelberg, no mourning ring this time. . . .

Now comes a sore point—my finances,[1] which

[1] Schumann's frequent complaints of being pinched for money need not be taken too seriously. Very few of the great German artists started life in such comfortable circumstances.

are in a bad way, and Heaven knows I have debts too. I wish I could show you those precious documents, my tailor's bill and my bootmaker's, to take only two. The tailor has had 90 florins from me since Easter, and I still owe him 55. My cloak was 85 florins, and two pairs of black trousers 36 florins. I have also had my blue dress-coat and my black coat turned, and had to have a tourist suit, to say nothing of other repairs. The bootmaker's case is not much better. In his bill a pair of Alpine boots looms large among various other pairs, and a pair of shoes among various repairs and re-solings—a melancholy array. Then I must eat, drink, play the piano, smoke, drive to Mannheim once in a way, go to lectures, buy books and music; and all this is a sad expense. Then there are these confounded dances (entailing fancy dress), tips, my subscription to the Museum, cigars (a serious item), the piano-tuner, the laundress, the shoe-black, candles and soap, also the drinks I occasionally have to stand—all these things would drive me to despair, if I were not desperate already. For a month I have not had a farthing in my pocket, and I receive plenty of discreet hints and meaning glances when I go out, although up to now I have only had one dun, and he was quite civil.

I should not tell you all this but for my customary frankness, and my inability to keep anything from you; indeed, I should tell you the name of my sweetheart, if I had one. Therefore have no delusions about me, but love me none the less, my dear Mother. . . .

15.

To his Mother.

HEIDELBERG, *July* 1, 1830, 4 *a.m.*

. . . I expect you will like to have a little picture of my everyday life. Except for the touch of rime-frost with which jurisprudence sometimes chills my early morning, the days would be all sunshine, fresh and radiant as dewy flowers. The divine enthusiasm of youth is a question of temperament, and not of age; consequently, people of the right sort, like yourself and the poets, are always young. My own simple idyll is compounded of music, jurisprudence, and poetry; poetry is to the prose of life as the shining gold setting to the hard, glittering diamond. I get up early, work from four to seven, sit at the piano from seven to nine, and am then off to Thibaut. The afternoon is divided between lectures and lessons or reading in English and Italian; the evening I spend with friends or out of doors. There you have the whole truth, and nothing but the truth. I feel sometimes that I am not a practical person, but Providence alone is responsible for that, since it endowed me with imagination to unravel and illuminate the tangled problems of the future. You may be sure I should like to be great in my profession, and I am really not wanting in good-will and energy. My failure to rise above the average will be no fault of mine, but of circumstances; perhaps, also, of my own heart, to which Latin has always been quite alien. Chance alone, or some heaven-sent turn of fortune, may lift the dark curtain which veils my future. Thibaut, for instance, does not encourage me to pursue my law studies, because, as he says, I was 'not born a bureaucrat,' and real efficiency is unattainable without native inclination. No automatic, machine-made lawyer, therefore, can excel in his profession. I cannot withhold from you these, my real convictions. But do not be alarmed; I have endless plans for the future, should this or that come to naught. . . .

16.

To his Mother.

HEIDELBERG, *July* 30, 1830, 5 *a.m.*

GOOD MORNING, MAMMA!

How shall I describe to you my bliss at this moment! The spirit-lamp is flaming and spluttering under the coffee-pot; there is an adorably clear golden sky, and the spirit of the morning is abroad in all its freshness. Then your letter lies before me, revealing a perfect mine of affection, sagacity, and virtue; my cigar has an excellent flavour; and, in short, the world is very fair at times—at least, to early risers.

My life here does not lack sunshine and blue sky, but I miss my cicerone, Rosen. The von H.'s, two brothers from Pomerania, whom I knew well, left for Italy a week ago; so I am left much to my own devices—that is, I am very happy or very miserable, as the fit takes me. Then, too, I sometimes work myself into a fever as I think over my past. My life has been for twenty years one long struggle between poetry and prose, or, let us say, music and law. My aims were as high in practical life as in art. I hoped to find scope for my energies and my powers of overcoming difficulties in a wide sphere of work. But what prospects are there, particularly in Saxony, for an ordinary plebeian, who has neither interest nor fortune, nor any real love for pettifogging legal details? At Leipzig I never troubled myself about my career, but dreamed and pottered away my time without any tangible results; here I have worked better, but my stay in both places has only tended to strengthen my leaning towards art. Now I stand at the cross-roads, trembling before the question, Whither? My own instinct points to art, and I believe it to be the right road, but it has always seemed to me—you will not be hurt if I whisper it lovingly—that you rather barred my way in that direction. I quite see your excellent motherly reasons, known to both of us as 'a precarious future' and 'an uncertain livelihood.' But let us look a little further. A man can know no greater torment than to look forward to an unhappy, empty, and lifeless future of his own planning; but neither is it easy for him to choose a profession directly opposed to that for which he was destined from his youth. Such a change means patience, confidence, and a rapid training.

My fancy is young, and sheds its halo over the artist-life; I have also arrived at the certainty that, given a good teacher and six years' steady, hard work, I shall be able to hold my own against any pianist, for pianoforte-playing is merely a matter of mechanical perfection. I have, besides, an occasional flight of fancy, and what is perhaps a real inspiration to compose. This brings me to the question—which shall I choose? I can only make my mark in one or the other. I tell myself that if I give my whole mind to a thing I am bound to succeed, dear Mother, in the end, through steady application. Thus the battle within rages more fiercely than ever. Sometimes I am foolhardy, and confident in my own tenacity; at others, doubtful, when I think of the immense stretch of road before me which I might by this time have covered. As for Thibaut, he has long been advising me to take up music. I should be very glad if you would write to him, and I know he would be pleased. He went to Rome some time ago, so I shall not have another chance of seeing him.

If I keep to law it certainly means spending another winter here to attend Thibaut's lectures on the Pandects, which no law student can afford to miss. If I decide on music, I must as certainly leave here and return to Leipzig. I should be quite glad to go under Wieck, who knows me, and can gauge my capabilities. Later on I should want a year in Vienna, and, if possible, lessons from Moscheles. And now, dear Mother, one request which you will perhaps be glad to fulfil. *Will you write yourself to Wieck at Leipzig, and ask him plainly what he thinks of me and my scheme?*[1] Please let me have a speedy reply, telling me your decision, so that I can hasten my departure from Heidelberg, loath as I am to leave this paradise, my many friends, and my bright dreams. Enclose this letter in your own to Wieck, if you like. In any case the matter must be settled by Michaelmas; then I will work, vigorously and without regrets, at my chosen profession.

You will admit that this is the most important letter I have ever written, or am likely to write. I hope you will not mind doing what I ask. Please answer as soon as possible; there is no time to be lost. Farewell, my dear Mother, and do not be anxious. It is a clear case of 'Heaven helps those who help themselves,' you see.

17.

To Friedrich Wieck.

HEIDELBERG, *August* 21, 1830.

MY BEST OF MASTERS,

It has taken a long time for the tumult of my ideas to quiet down. What an upheaval the reading of those two letters caused! I am just beginning to feel more collected. I at once took

[1] His mother wrote to Wieck, who replied that he thought he could guarantee Schumann's success as a pianist, if he persevered, practised sufficiently, and was willing to undergo a course of theoretical studies.

courage on reading your letter, and concluded that Atlas was overthrown. In his place stood a child of the Sun, pointing to the east, saying, 'Beware of thwarting Nature, lest thy good genius take his flight for ever. The road to science lies over ice-clad mountains; the road to art also lies over mountains, but they are tropical, set with flowers, hopes, and dreams.' Such was the state of my feelings on first reading your letter and my mother's, but I am much calmer now. . . .

I choose art, and by this decision I will, can, and must abide. I can bid good-bye without a tear to a science which I do not love and barely respect; but it is not without qualms that I look down the long vista leading to the goal I have set myself. I assure you I am modest, as, indeed, I have reason to be; but I am also courageous, patient, trusting, and teachable. I put myself in your hands with entire confidence. Take me as I am, and be patient with me in everything. Reproaches shall not depress me, nor praise make me idle. A few bucketfuls of cold, real cold, theory will not hurt me, and I shall not dodge the wetting. I have carefully read and considered your five 'but's'; I have asked myself severely if I can satisfy them; and in each case my reason and my inclination answer: 'Yes, without a doubt.' Take my hand and lead me, honoured Master, for I will follow you blindly; and never shift the bandage from my eyes, lest they be dazzled by the splendour. If I could show you my inner self at this moment, you would see me at peace in a world bathed with the fragrance of the dawn.

You may rely upon me. Your pupil shall be worthy of the name. Ah, Master, can you tell me why we are sometimes so blissfully happy in this world? I know the secret! . . .

18.

To his Mother.

HEIDELBERG, *August* 22, 1830.

MY ADORED MOTHER,

The 19th of August, which brought me letters from you all, was a wonderful day. My inmost self was called upon to weigh my future in the balance and to choose the rising scale. But I did not find the choice difficult, in spite of the gravity of the decision on which my whole future, my fame, my happiness—and perhaps yours—depend.

Believe me, I fully appreciate your loving tenderness, and was led by your doubts to probe deeper into myself than I otherwise should have done. But you may be sure I have passed my whole life in review during the last few days to help me in my decision.

But whether I put the question to my head, heart, or reason, view it in the light of past, present, or future, or according to my abilities, hopes, or prospects, everything from my childhood onwards points to an artistic career. Ask yourself frankly, as you think over my childhood, boyhood, and early manhood, in what direction my instincts always led me. Remember how my father's clear-sighted intelligence destined me at that early age for art or music. . . . You yourself in the letter before this dwell on my devotion to poetry, nature, music, etc. Beware of thwarting nature and your own genius, lest you offend both irrevocably. . . . Let me draw you a parallel, and for the present leave everything to Wieck: you have reason to trust him.

The signpost pointing towards Art says: 'If you are diligent you can reach your goal in three years.' Law says: 'In three years you may, perhaps, be an *accessist* earning sixteen *groschen* a year.' Art continues: 'I am free as air, and the whole world is my haven.' Law says with a shrug: 'My practice involves constant subordination at every step of the way, and immaculate dress.' Art goes on to say: 'Where I am, there is beauty; I rule the heart, whose emotions I have called into being; I am unshackled and infinite; I compose and am immortal,' etc. Law says sternly: 'I have nothing to offer but musty deeds, village squabbles, or, with exceptional luck, the exciting mystery of a sudden death. I cannot consider editing new Pandects,' etc. . . .

I will not turn the conversation on to baser considerations, such as the comparative lucrativeness of the two professions, since the answer is self-evident.

Dearest Mother, I can only give you a slight and fleeting sketch of all that I have thought out so thoroughly. I wish you were with me and could read my thoughts. I know you would say: 'Enter on your new career with courage, diligence and confidence, and you will not fall.' Give me your hands, dear people, and let me go my way. I assure you we have all more reason to face the future cheerfully now than we had before.

Eduard's proposal is good and kind, but it will not do, for the loss of six months is far more serious to me in my art than in law, where I can so easily make it good. But Wieck's proposal is capital. He says: 'Let Robert come to me for six months on trial.' So be it. If Wieck gives a favourable report, then I may safely hope to make progress and win fame. On the other hand, if he has any shadow of doubt after those six months, there is still no harm done. I can study another year, take my examination, and shall even then only have studied four years. . . .

PART II

FLORESTAN AND EUSEBIUS

'Eusebius's mildness, Florestan's ire—
I can give thee, at will, my tears or my fire,
For my soul by turns two spirits possess—
The spirits of joy and of bitterness.'

From SCHUMANN'S *verses to* CLARA.

'Florestan and Eusebius form my dual nature; I should like to melt them into the perfect man, Raro.'

To HEINRICH DORN, *September* 14, 1836.

19.

To his Mother.

LEIPZIG, *October* 25, 1830.

I should have written ages ago, but had literally neither pen nor paper. I have been homeless in Leipzig for a fortnight, and am in consequence too irritable and unsettled to collect my thoughts.

If you only knew what your letters are to me, the last especially, in which I hardly know whether the human or the motherly element most moves my admiration. In the first flush of my delight I went to Wieck. 'How far superior is your Mother to your guardian!' he said; and I repeated some more to him. Continue to be gentle with me, dear Mother. . . .

Will you send me, some time, *all* my letters to you? They would be useful to me in some work I am doing. I should like to see, too, whether I have changed much in these two years and a half. Please send them.

20.

To his Mother.

LEIPZIG, *November* 15, 1830.

Three of your letters lie before me unanswered. First of all, my best thanks for everything—beds, linen, coffee, etc. The coffee in particular was a source of much simple idyllic pleasure. Flechsig always had his coffee sent in bottles from Zwickau, and this unromantic attention pleased me so much at the time that I thought I would write for some too. Julius is right about the sealing-wax; I did not think of it. You are perfectly right about the cigars, but I really think I smoke less than I used. I should not go so far as to call it a passion. Last time I travelled I did not smoke fifty, and had no great hankering after them. In other ways I am retrenching as far as I can, but one extravagance remains—I still burn two candles in the evening. I have been to see Barth,[1] but have not yet paid my Sunday call. Sometimes I could sacrifice all considerations to my odious moodiness and mis-

[1] J. A. Barth, a Leipzig bookseller and publisher.

anthropic indifference. The Caruses[1] insist on introducing me to numerous families, thinking it 'good for my career.' I am sure it would be, and yet I don't go; indeed, I hardly leave my room. I am often heavy, dull, and disagreeable; my laughter is of a sardonic order, and there is hardly a trace of my old heartiness and enthusiasm. You will not enjoy my company at Christmas. You say you were incapable of praying after you had read my letter, telling you of my decision. Can that be really true? I shall not be much satisfaction to you as I am, but I vow that if I stuck to law I should shoot myself from sheer boredom when I became a junior barrister. . . .

21.

To his Mother.

LEIPZIG, *December* 15, 1830.

You write as youthfully as my own Jean Paul in this letter; every word is a flower. If the glorious time in which we live, in which even greybeards renew their youth, does not quite eclipse the star of art, I shall not be afraid of appearing in the encyclopædias and 'Portraits of Celebrated Men,' or of seeing our whole El Dorado of letters in print. How we shall figure as son and mother! You don't know how such letters as yours refresh me, with what new strength and

[1] E. A. Carus, M.D., a Leipzig professor, who knew Schumann's uncle at Zwickau. His wife was an admirable singer, from whom Schumann first heard Schubert's songs.

energy they inspire me in the constant struggle towards my goal! Kindly encouragement gives me power of resistance, and new, far-reaching courage. 'You have your true love, your true friend, in joy or sorrow. Ah! music bestows a sweet, soothing consolation which words cannot give. Do you in your turn be true to her whom you have chosen as the comrade of your earthly existence.' Words like these linger long in the memory, especially when they are the expression of a mother's emotion. But I shall be faithful, even should my mistress prove faithless. I could write a great deal more to-day, but my hand shakes, and I feel I must walk up and down the room, and think of the snowflakes which a breath of spring is scattering.

The 15th, Evening.

I sometimes feel quite well and happy. I work hard, and am getting on famously; in three or four years I hope to be ready for Moscheles.[1] Do you remember how we sat together at a concert at Carlsbad, and you whispered to me joyfully that Moscheles was sitting behind us, and then how every one made way for him, and how modestly he carried himself? I mean to take him for my model in everything. Believe me, dearest Mother, with patience and endurance I can accomplish much if I will. I sometimes lack confidence in public, although I am proud enough inwardly. I pray

[1] Ignaz Moscheles (1794-1870), the pianist. He lived in London from 1821 onwards.

God I may keep myself strong, modest, steady, and sober. The flame that is naturally clear always gives the most light and heat. If I could blend my talent for poetry and music into one, the light would burn still clearer, and I might go far.

I cannot bear the idea now of dying in philistinism; I feel I must always have been destined for music. Do you know, I always stole the hours when you went to see Mrs. Ruppius for composing? Ah, those happy hours! I shall have many more of them. Your indirect invitation for New Year's Eve is more inviting than any request or demand for my presence. This letter would be sufficient to bring me, were there no other inducement. I shall perhaps fly over for a few minutes, and play you a few pranks, like a zephyr in winter. Until then, hang up this picture of me.

But I must thank you, too, for the remittance. My indifference to money and my spendthrift ways are disgraceful. You have no idea how reckless I am; how often I practically throw money out of the window. I am always making good resolutions, but the next minute I forget and give the waiter eightpence. Living away from home and travelling have much to do with it, but I have to blame chiefly myself and my cursed recklessness. No cure for it, I'm afraid.

It was only a joke about my looking pale and wretched. I am as blooming as a rose, and as healthy as a fish. I occasionally have toothache.

See the portrait! My Weimar scheme[1] is grand. How, in Heaven's name, can you say it might be too expensive? There is time enough, for I must at all costs finish my course with Wieck. The other day I threw out a careless hint about the Hummel plan, but he was offended, and asked if I mistrusted him, or whose doing it was. Was he not the best living teacher? I showed my alarm at his sudden outburst, but we have made it up again, and he treats me like his own child. You have no conception of his enthusiasm, his critical judgment of art; but where his own interests or Clara's are at stake, he is as savage and intractable as a boor. . . .

22.

To his Mother.

May 15, 1831.

. . . All this long time I have not been able to collect my thoughts sufficiently to write you a long letter. It will not be of a rosy hue, either. I have kept my room almost entirely for six days. I have pain in my stomach, my heart, my head—oh, everywhere! Otherwise I am in unusually good spirits. For three successive days I had to undergo a régime of perspiration, under the doctor's orders. My hand trembles as I write. I have a touch of cholera or something of that sort; but I hope to be on my legs again, and with you, dear

[1] Schumann had told his mother of his intention of going to Weimar, to become a pupil of Hummel (*cf.* Letter 23). He tried to persuade her to remove to Weimar also.

Mother, by the 1st of June. Are you really as kind as ever? Your last words at our leave-taking will ever live in my memory. When I say them over to myself, it is as if my good genius folded me in his arms. I have become so suspicious that I can hardly be too often assured of my friends' affection. . . .

And so I potter along. Like all young, impulsive people, I make the mistake of trying to be everything at once, and this only complicates my work and unsettles my mind. But as I grow older I shall be calmer and more level-headed. There are but four courses open to me: conducting, teaching, playing, and composition. Hummel, of course, combines all four; I shall probably turn to the two last. I must really give up dabbling in many things, and aim at excellence in one. My success depends chiefly on my power to live a persistently clean, sober, and reputable life. If I hold fast by this, my good genius, who fairly possesses me at times, will not desert me. . . .

23.

To J. N. Hummel, at Weimar.[1]

LEIPZIG, *August* 20, 1831.

DEAR SIR,

My intimate acquaintance with your compositions, which is of many years' standing, must

[1] Johann Nepomuk Hummel (1778-1837) had conducted the Weimar court orchestra since 1819, and was considered the first authority on pianoforte teaching. Schumann's estimate of his compositions was afterwards modified, but Hummel is certainly underrated in our day.

be the excuse for this intrusive letter from a stranger. More than once, as I realized the full beauty of your tone-pictures, did the desire arise to know the man who has given to the world such exquisite moments, though I little thought I should ever have an opportunity. But I am assured on all sides that a student may go to a great master for advice with no fear of a rebuff, and am therefore encouraged to approach you.

Before venturing on a request, the fulfilment of which I leave entirely to your judgment, permit me, dear sir, to explain the object of this letter. From my earliest childhood I have had a passionate love for music, though the fact that I sat at the piano all day and improvised proves nothing. My father, a bookseller in a provincial town and a man of unusual perspicacity, was perhaps quicker to perceive my musical bent than my mother, who, anxious as all mothers are, preferred a so-called bread-winning profession to the thorny path of art. It is true there was some question of my studying with Director von Weber,[1] but a delay was caused by his absence in England up to the time when death deprived me of my father in 1826. I was thus left to follow my own instincts without guidance. There was no one I could take as my pattern in the small town, where, indeed, I possibly figured as such myself. Three years ago I entered the university here, troubling myself but little as to my destiny or my future profession. I attended

[1] Karl Maria von Weber.

a few lectures, and also zealously pursued my studies in pianoforte-playing and composition under good masters. To give you an idea of the vigorous reforms my teacher had to institute, I must tell you that, although I could play any concerto at sight, I had to go back and learn the scale of C major. But my progress was encouraging, and I worked so hard that I was able, after a year, to play *the* A minor concerto (there is only one) with ease and certainty and with technical correctness. I even played it once or twice in public. At Easter, 1829, I went to Heidelberg, travelled subsequently for some time in Switzerland and Italy, and returned to Heidelberg at Easter, 1830. Then, all at once, the thought seized me: what are you going to make of your life? I had better say nothing of the struggle which followed. It lasted nearly six months, the outcome being my decision to devote myself to art. I requested my mother to write to Wieck at Leipzig, and ask him what he thought of my prospects as a musician. His answer was encouraging; he pointed out that, as I was not quite without means, I had less need than some others to take into account the precariousness of an artist's livelihood.

The step was taken, and I returned to Leipzig fired with enthusiasm and armed with the firmest resolves. But what a change did I find in my old master! Contrary to his former method of weighing each note critically and studying each movement conscientiously page by page, he let me scramble through good and bad alike, neglecting both touch and fingering. His one idea was to secure a brilliant, Paganini-like performance, and I could hardly play splashily enough to please him. My master wished to rid me of a certain cautious, mechanical, studied manner of playing, and I can imagine that this method might succeed better with his daughter, who indeed shows wonderful promise, but I am not ripe for such bold treatment. I quite realize that this year at Leipzig has widened my views on execution, conception, and so on, but has advanced me very little in the direction of a real mastery of the art.

I now appeal to the Master in the hope that he will allow me to profit by his teaching for a time. My dear mother, desirous of my success, joins me in this request. Her whole confidence goes out to one who is celebrated for his kindness to young artists.

I venture to enclose the first solo of a concerto,[1] which will indicate more clearly than any description my present stage. I may explain that this bold attempt at writing in concerto form is not my first effort in composition; I have tried my hand at great and small, and the concerto form seemed to me easier than that of the sonata, for instance, because of its greater license.

I have written, dear Sir, freely, and asked much, for which I can only offer in return my poor thanks in anticipation. My long-cherished desire for your

[1] For pianoforte in F.

acquaintance and my passionate devotion to music must supply the place of further excuses.

If ever I closed a letter with a feeling of genuine respect, it is this.[1]

24.

To his Brother, Julius Schumann.

LEIPZIG, *September* 5, 1831.

MY DEAR BROTHER,

I must confess to you my painful, almost childish, dread of cholera, and my fear that a sudden seizure may put an end to my existence. The thought of dying now, at twenty, before I have done anything except spend money, maddens me. I have been in a fever for days, making a thousand plans, only to dismiss and revive them alternately. In an epidemic I consider flight a duty, unless it causes too great a disturbance to our friends; and as there is no danger of that in my case, I should very much like to be off to sunny Italy for six months or so, or to Augsburg for a time with Wieck (who is going on to Paris with

[1] In reply Hummel wrote encouragingly about Schumann's compositions, although he evidently considered that he was in danger of sacrificing too much to originality. Schumann was afterwards advised on all sides not to study under Hummel, who was becoming old-fashioned; but he was convinced that Hummel's reputation would be useful to him in Vienna, where he proposed to settle eventually. In a letter to his mother (May 5, 1832) he announces his intention of going to him at Michaelmas, but by that time he was obliged to give up the idea of being a pianist, on account of his lamed hand. [Tr.]

Probst[1]), or to Hummel at Weimar. On the other hand, I should really prefer staying here, as I don't want to travel, and am getting on with my music. Altogether, I am in such a desperate state of agitation and indecision that I almost feel like putting a bullet through my head. . . .

25.

To his Mother.

LEIPZIG, *September* 21, 1831.

. . . I am not going to Weimar at present. The fact is, I shall shortly become the father of a fine, healthy infant, whom I should like to see christened before I leave Leipzig. The child will make its appearance at Probst's. How I hope you will understand its child's message of youth and life![2] If you did but know the first joys of authorship! Being engaged can be nothing to it. What hopes and prophetic visions fill my soul's heaven! The Doge of Venice, as he wedded the sea, was not prouder than I, as I celebrate my nuptials with the great world within whose vast range the artist may roam or rest at will. Is it not a consoling thought that this first leaf of my fancy which flutters into ether may find its way to some sore heart, bringing balm to soothe its pain and heal its wound? . . .

[1] Probst had a music-shop at Leipzig.

[2] Variations on the name Abegg, Op. 1.

26.

To Friedrich Wieck, at Frankfurt-am-Main.

LEIPZIG, *January* 11, 1832.

I might, my dear friend and Master, begin this letter as if it were a continuation, for I write to you every hour in spirit. To-day I at last sit down firmly determined not to lay aside my pen until the letter is done. First let me congratulate you warmly on Clara's success.[1] Indeed, the public, which forgets so easily, seldom overlooks anything really remarkable, though I am sometimes tempted to compare it to a herd of cattle momentarily distracted by the lightning from its peaceful grazing. Schubert, Paganini, and Chopin have flashed across the horizon, and now comes—Clara.

You cannot believe how I long to be back with you both! I need to be with people who will draw me upward to a higher level. I am so apt to be proud and cynical with my equals or with people from whom I can admit no criticism. I shall never agree with Dorn,[2] who is bent on persuading me

[1] Wieck had taken Clara on an extended concert tour, commencing on September 25. They had given successful concerts at Weimar (where they were received by Goethe), Erfurt, Gotha, Arnstadt, and Kassel, and were, at the time when Schumann wrote, in very low spirits, on account of their poor reception at Frankfurt. Their tour ended with Paris, where they stayed two months.

[2] Heinrich Dorn (1804-1892) was at Leipzig from 1829 to 1832 in the course of his eventful career as a conductor, which closed with his summons to the Court Opera in Berlin (1849-1869).

that a fugue is the whole of music. How very differently people are constituted! Yet I admit that the theoretical studies have done me good; for where I was once content to transfer to paper the impulse of the moment, I now stand critically aside to watch the play of my inspiration, pausing now and again to take my bearings. I wonder if you ever passed through this kind of a haze yourself. There are, as I think, some who, like Mozart, never experience it; others, like Hummel, steer their way through; others, again, like Schubert, never come out of it; while some can even laugh at it with Beethoven.

And now, how are you? Do not be alarmed at a certain incoherence in this letter, for I have so much to tell you that I hardly know where to begin.

Chopin's Op. 1 (which I firmly believe to be Op. 10 at least) lies before me. A lady might call it quite pretty and piquant, rather like Moscheles. But I think you will let Clara learn it, for it is full of inspiration, and presents few difficulties. I modestly maintain, however, that it is separated from Op. 2 by a period of two years and a score of other compositions. . . .

27.

To Clara Wieck (enclosed in the above).

My very dear Clara,

I could hardly repress a smile yesterday when I read in the *Didaskalia* that 'Fräulein Clara

Wieck' had been playing variations by Herz, etc. Forgive this levity, my dear Fräulein, but surely the best title is—none at all. Who would say Herr Paganini or Herr Goethe? I know you are of a thoughtful turn, and understand your crazy old inventor of charades. You are to me, my dear Clara, not a sister or a girl friend, but the pilgrim's distant shrine. While you have been away I have been to Arabia for fairy tales likely to please you. There are six new ones of a man haunted by his double, a hundred and one charades, eight droll riddles, some delightfully creepy robber tales, and a white ghost story, which positively makes me shudder. Alwin[1] has grown into quite a nice boy. His new blue overcoat and his leather cap, which is just like mine, suit him uncommonly well. There is no startling news of Gustav, except that he has grown so tremendously that you will hardly know him. . . . Clemens is the drollest little fellow, very lovable and very obstinate. He talks like a book, and has the most sonorous voice. He has grown a good deal too. Alwin's violin will run away with him one of these days. . . . Have you been composing vigorously? And if so, what? In my dreams I sometimes hear music—it must be yours.

I am now doing three-part fugue with Dorn, besides which I have finished a sonata in B minor

[1] Alwin (1821-1885) was Clara's brother by Friedrich Wieck's first marriage, as was Gustav. Clemens was a son of Wieck's second marriage. The two latter died in childhood.

and a book of *Papillons*, which will appear within the next fortnight—in print! Dorn is giving a concert a month from now. The Polish concert was so full that three hundred people had to be turned away. The weather is glorious to-day. How do apples taste at Frankfurt? And how is the top F in that skipping variation of Chopin's? My paper is coming to an end, like everything else except the friendship which preserves to Fräulein Clara Wieck

HER WARMEST ADMIRER.

28.

To Heinrich Dorn.

LEIPZIG, *April* 25, 1832.

DEAR HERR DIRECTOR,

What can have induced you to break off our relations so suddenly? I ought not to wonder that your patience gave way before my incessant pleas for indulgence and forgiveness, yet I never thought that you would desert me so near the goal. It is only since I have helped two of my friends as far as syncopations that I realize the thoroughness and infallibility of your method. Some of the side-issues upon which you casually touched (intervals, for instance) seemed to me quite clear at the time, though I now see that I was far from understanding them. You must not think I have been stagnating or idling since you left me, but it seems as if I could only assimilate ideas I evolve for myself, so strongly does my whole nature resent any outside stimulus. So I have been going cautiously forward from where we left off (using Marpurg), and have not, I confess, given up the hope of studying canon again with you some day. I now see the inestimable value of theoretical studies; it is only the abuse of them which is harmful. I have missed your help very much in adapting Paganini's Caprices for the pianoforte, as the basses were often doubtful, but I overcame the difficulty by choosing the simplest. Besides these, I have finished six intermezzi with trios and a prelude and fugue (a triple fugue, if you please!), which I should like to show you. And now, if I ask my conscience whom this letter was written to please, I am bound to reply: myself. Am I not an egoist?

But I hope, all the same, you will forgive and make excuses for

YOUR FAITHFUL PUPIL.

29.

To his Mother.

LEIPZIG, *May* 8, 1832.

I have just been reading over your last three letters, two of which date from January, to see if I had forgotten to answer anything in them. I should like to send you some extracts from my commonplace-book, which should both enlighten you as to my thoughts and doings during the past months and perhaps excuse my silence; but the entries during this period are exceptionally scanty and unimportant. 'An artist must maintain a nice adjustment in his relations with the outside world, otherwise he is bound to go under.' This is what I tried to do first of all. Consequently, my attention has been turned inward in the absence of the distraction once offered by travelling and gayer surroundings. And, since your son is as incapable of moderation in right as in wrong doing, this self-observation or spying on my own sensations developed into a form of hypochondria, which prevented a clear conception of my future position, and was in itself depressing and unsettling. Then, too, keenly as I am attracted by art in its manifold expression and its unceasing endeavour, I was often vain enough to think that I did not play a sufficiently important part in practical everyday life. I retired still further into myself, examined my past life thoroughly, and vainly tried to arrive at some clear understanding of my aim and my scope, of what I had accomplished and of what I had become. But I soon decided that just as excess or misuse of the finest and noblest things produces satiety and indifference, so does intelligent, conscientious, persevering work alone secure progress, and preserve the charm in any art, especially in music. The stronger the original impulse, the greater is the reaction. For another thing, I have long been dissatisfied with my social life. Wieck, the one person whose company I sought and enjoyed, our interest being mutual, has been in Paris. Lühe[1]

[1] Willibald von der Lühe (born 1800), formerly an officer, was then living at Leipzig, where he wrote and published several works of reference.

used to come every day, but his conventional views, clever as they are, prevented me from really fraternizing with him. Moritz Semmel, whom I respect for his discernment, resolution, and devotion to his work, proved a pleasanter companion in brighter moods; but the wide divergence of our individual aims led to a breach, the more inexplicable as we could have supplied one another's deficiencies. I was thus left more and more alone, and reached, at times, a deadlock from which I was only set free by *my innate aversion to every form of idleness.*

Two of my compositions have just been published, and I missed Wieck, whose judgment is so rarely biased that I set great store by it in some respects. My theoretical studies with Dorn have been of great value in bringing my mind, through steady application, to a state of clearness, after which I have often dimly striven. My life has changed; I am independent. Realizing my new responsibilities, I hesitated to part with the MS. Well, it is printed now, for all the world to see and judge. Some few criticisms have reached my ears, indulgent, appreciative, or censorious. . . . Many a sleepless night has brought before me a vision of my goal as a distant picture; and, as I wrote the *Papillons,*[1] I could feel the stirring of a certain independence, but this is precisely what most of the critics reject. As I watch my *Papillons* fluttering in the spring air, as I see spring itself looking in at my door, a

[1] Op. 2, dedicated to his three sisters-in-law. [Tr.]

child with eyes of heaven's blue, I begin to comprehend the meaning of my existence. The silence is broken; my letter is in your hands. . . .

To give you a faithful picture of my domestic life I should have to paint the morning in the Italian, the evening in the Dutch manner. My lodgings are respectable, roomy and comfortable. I spring out of bed, nimble as a deer, at about five o'clock, and devote myself to my accounts, my diary and my correspondence. Then I work, compose or read a little by turns, up to eleven, when Lühe appears with the utmost regularity. He is, indeed, a perfect model of order and punctuality. Then comes dinner, after which I read a little French or a newspaper. From three to six I generally take a solitary walk, usually the road to Connewitz. Its beauty leads me to ask myself and you: can we not have our heaven on earth if we take a simple, sober view of life, and are not unreasonable in our demands? I sometimes clap my hands for joy as I tell myself that I need not go to America to find true happiness. If I am home by six I improvise until nearly eight, then have supper with [Kömpel] and Wolff as a rule, and come home again.

But, as I wish to be perfectly open with you, dear Mother, I confess unblushingly that this routine was frequently upset during February and March; interruptions became, indeed, rather the rule than the exception. You asked Rascher yourself whether I really drank much, and he, I believe, defended me. I could not have defended myself, for there was truth in the accusation. But as drinking Bavarian beer must be accounted a prosaic habit rather than a poetic passion, it was not easy to give it up, for it is infinitely simpler to cure a passion than an old habit. If you ask whether I have given it up, I can answer confidently in the affirmative. . . .

30.

To his Mother.

LEIPZIG, *August* 9, 1832.

My whole house is turned into a chemist's shop. The fact is, I began to feel uneasy about my hand,[1] though I assiduously avoided consulting a surgeon, for fear the dreaded blow should fall in his verdict: 'incurable.' I began to make all sorts of plans for the future—decided to study theology in place of law, and even arrived at adorning my parsonage with living pictures of yourself and others! In the end I went to Professor Kühl, and asked him, on his honour, whether it would come right. After shaking his head a few times, he said: 'Yes, but not for some time—say six months.' Once I had this assurance, the weight fell from my heart, and I joyfully followed out all his instructions. They were bad enough, for they spelt *Tierbäder* (let Schurig tell you what they are)—bathing my hand

[1] Schumann had tried to obtain independent action of the fingers by fastening up the middle finger in a sling, and playing only with the other four. As a result, he lost the use of the finger completely.

constantly in warm brandy-and-water by day and poulticing it with herbs at night, and as little playing as possible. It is not the most charming of cures, and I fear something of the bovine element will pass into my temperament, though I confess the baths are very strengthening. Altogether, I feel so strong and fit that I have a healthy desire to thrash some one. But what nonsense I am talking! Forgive me, dear Mother. I need hardly say that a journey to Zwickau is out of the question under these circumstances. But come and see whether your boy would receive you with open arms if you paid him a visit! You could not stay with me, as Eduard knows; but why not go to the hotel? You can have splendid rooms very cheaply by the month. It would certainly be the most comfortable arrangement, and I would see to everything for you. Would not Emilia[1] come too, either to stay or simply to bear you company? I really long to see her again.

My journey to Vienna has to be postponed on the same account. If my cure succeeds, I shall go there, after paying you a visit. It is better not to go to Dresden until name and reputation are assured, for it is a hard matter to acquire them there. Reissiger[2] does not attract me; his way is so different from mine. Music is to me the perfect expression of the soul, while to some it is a

[1] His brother Julius's wife.

[2] Karl Gottfried Reissiger (1798-1859) had been director of the German opera at Dresden since 1826.

mere intoxication of the sense of hearing, and to others an arithmetical problem, and treated as such. You are quite right to insist that every man should aim at contributing to the common weal; but, let me add, he must not sink to the common level. Climbing brings us to the top of the ladder. I have no desire to be understood by the common herd. . . .

31.

To his Mother.

LEIPZIG, *November* 6, 1832,
at 2 a.m. precisely.

What a lot of pleasant things I have to tell you to-day! First of all, we shall certainly meet within a fortnight. The thought of this has been keeping me so wide awake all night that I decided to get up and write or study. Then, Wieck is giving a concert at Zwickau with Clara, and, actually, a symphony movement of mine is to be included in the programme. You must let this account for my long silence, dear Mother. For the last fortnight I have worked incessantly, and am beginning to wonder if I shall really be ready in time. I have given up my rooms for two months (if you can do with me for so long), and have let my piano to Lühe for that time. Everything, in fact, is ready for the journey except the symphony. One thing distresses me: I still owe about fifty talers, which I do not know how to raise. If you or my brothers could spare this amount just now, it would be a great relief to me. Please let me have an answer by return without fail. As for my hand, the doctor still tries to console me; *but I have quite given up hope*, believing it to be incurable. At Zwickau I shall take up the violoncello again, for which I only need my left-hand fingers. It is most helpful, too, in symphony-writing. Meanwhile the right hand will have rest, which is the medicine it needs. My theological plan,[1] by the way, was merely an idea which came to me in my momentary state of depression. The inclination no longer exists, I may say. I am really behaving quite nicely, and if my present steady working mood lasts, *you need have no fear for the future*. How I am looking forward to seeing you, dearest, best of Mothers! One thing more—if I am silent at times, do not think me dissatisfied or melancholy. I never talk much when I am really absorbed in my ideas, my book, or my emotions. I have received civilities, gratification, and encouragement from various quarters lately.

Clara will give you much to think about. Wieck is, like myself, counting upon Eduard's piano Please ask him and Theresa beforehand in my name and Wieck's. I owe him so much.

Farewell, dearest Mother.

32.

To his Mother.

LEIPZIG, *June* 28, 1833.

. . . And now, to tell you of myself. My life has not been without charm and interest since I

[1] See Letter 30.

wrote. I have taken my own little band of congenial spirits, mostly music students, with me to swell Wieck's circle. We are principally concerned with a plan for bringing out a new musical paper,[1] which Hofmeister is to publish. Prospectuses and notices will be out next month. The whole thing is to be fresher and more varied in tone than the existing papers, and we aim at avoiding the conventional routine at all costs. But I see little prospect of agreeing with Wieck's ideas on art, in spite of his daily increasing friendliness towards me. The more brains, the more ideas, even though they clash! The directors are Ortlepp, Wieck, myself, and two other professors—nearly all fine players (except this poor nine-fingered creature), and this of itself stamps the thing as differing from the amateurishness of other musical papers. Among our other contributors I may mention Lühe, Councillor Wendt, Lyser (who is deaf), Reissiger and Krägen at Dresden, and Franz Otto[2] in London. This undertaking may possibly give me the necessary basis for an assured social standing, which would be to my character what the frame is to the picture, or a vessel to its fluid

[1] The *Neue Zeitschrift für Musik*. The first number appeared April 3, 1834. Schumann's literary activity dates back to 1831, when his enthusiastic notice of Chopin's *Don Juan* variations appeared. He had already evolved the Eusebius-Florestan idea.

[2] Wendt (1783-1836), Professor of Philosophy; J. P. Lyser (1803-1870); Karl Krägen (1797-1879), of Dresden; Franz Otto (1809-1842), a popular writer of part-songs for male voices.

contents. Like many another artist, I long to attain this, and have an instinctive distaste for an undefined position. I will say nothing of the eventual financial advantages, etc. . . .

Eduard will probably have told you that I have seen a good deal of Kalkbrenner,[1] that most courteous and amiable of Frenchmen, whose vanity is his only fault. Now that I am acquainted with all the principal virtuosi except Hummel, I begin to realize that my own achievements were once considerable. These great people, instead of offering us something new or original, as we expect, are too fond of giving us our own dear old errors under cover of fine names. I assure you, a name is half the battle. In my opinion none of these men will bear comparison with the two girl artists, Mlle. Belleville[2] and Clara. Clara, who is as fond of me as ever, is the same wild and fanciful little person, skipping and tearing about like a child one moment, and full of serious sayings the next. It is a pleasure to watch the increasing rapidity with which she unfolds the treasures of her heart and mind, as a flower unfolds its petals. The other day as we came home from Connewitz together—we do a two or three hours' tramp nearly every day—I heard her say to herself, 'Oh, how happy, how happy I am!' Who does not love to hear that? Along this same road there are some very unneces-

[1] Friedrich Kalkbrenner (1788-1849), an eminent pianist.

[2] Emilia von Belleville-Qury (1808-1880), one of Czerny's best pupils.

sary stones in the middle of the footpath. Now, I have a way of looking up, and not down, when I am talking, so she walks just behind me, and gently pulls my coat before every stone to keep me from falling, stumbling over them herself in between. . . .

33.

To Clara Wieck.

LEIPZIG, *August* 2, 1833.

DEAR CLARA,

To anyone who is not a flatterer there can be few things more unpalatable than writing or acknowledging letters of dedication.[1] The modesty, deprecation, and weight of gratitude one feels are indeed overwhelming. I should, for instance, in reply to anyone else, have to ask how I deserved such a distinction, and whether you had duly considered it; or I should resort to metaphor and say that the moon would be invisible to man did not the sun's rays illumine it at times; or, see how the noble vine twines itself about the lowly elm, nourishing the barren tree with its sap. But, as it is you and none other, I will only proffer my warmest thanks. If you were present, I should squeeze your hand, and that without asking your

[1] Clara Schumann gave proof, later in life, of her talent for composition. A pianoforte concerto (Op. 7) and several preludes and fugues (Op. 16) figured on her concert programmes. She collaborated with Robert in 'Twelve Songs by Rückert, composed by Robert and Clara Schumann' (Op. 12), providing, as her share, numbers 2, 4, and 11.

father's permission! I might also express a hope that the union of our names on the title-page may be symbolic of a union of our thoughts and ideas in the future. This is all a poor beggar like myself can do.

My work is probably doomed to remain a ruin, like many another, as the only progress I have made of late is in scratching out. But I am sending something else. Please say good morning to Krägen for me, and ask him if he will be godfather to the work; that is, if I may dedicate it to him.

As the weather is so very threatening to-day, I am afraid I must deny myself the pleasure of coming to you for music this evening. I have spun myself so snugly into my cocoon, too, that only the tips of my wings peep out, and they might so easily be bruised. In any case, I hope to see you again before you leave.

PART III

THE 'DAVIDSBÜNDLER'

'The *Davidsbund*[1] is, as you will have gathered, a spiritual and romantic league. Mozart was as much a member of it as Berlioz now is, or as you now are, without being enrolled in due form.' —*From a letter to* HEINRICH DORN, *September* 14, 1836.

34.

To Friedrich Wieck.

LEIPZIG, *August* 6, 1833.

. . . If I understood you aright, you said, 'Put all your heart into the matter, and I promise you my help, but if you grow lukewarm! . . .' I retire, were you going to say? Are you not co-editor of the paper, and, as such, willing to take your share of weal or woe? If you indeed cast in your lot with us, as your interest in the affair led me to

[1] The name 'Davidites' was invented by Schumann to include himself (in his various impersonations) and the friends whose sympathies were with him in his war against the Philistines, 'musical and otherwise.' Musical criticism, in particular, was on a very low level at this period, and the existing musical papers were lifeless and conventional. Schumann's own criticisms were signed 'Eusebius,' 'Florestan,' or occasionally 'Raro.' Eusebius would be filled with gentle enthusiasm over some new composition, while Florestan would

believe, can a supposed coolness on my part be any excuse for your falling-off? Is your support really so half-hearted?

To anyone with whose manner of speech I am less familiar, I should have answered bluntly: 'Take all the honours yourself; all I ask is that you apply the curb when my ardour runs away with me, while I, for my part, undertake to do the same by you. But it is only fair that you should lend me your spurs if I flag.' Am I, then, so greedy of fame, or so much in love with editorship—if, indeed, you dignify the charge of correspondence, etc., by that name? If you do not consider this the greatest possible sacrifice on my side, I shall not, of course, be able to convince you. I only undertake it because I am best acquainted with the circumstances, and because I am reluctant to give up an idea which is, I see, fraught with incalculable educational benefit both to mind and to heart.

But as I may claim to know your way of talking, and am possibly taking you too seriously, I prefer to understand you as expressing some doubt as to my future perseverance, which I recognize as reason-

---

ruthlessly reveal the faults which Eusebius had overlooked. Raro, with his sound judgment, was perhaps intended to personify Wieck. Schumann also provided his contributors with fanciful names when he enrolled them as Davidites. Thus, *Julius* was Knorr; *Jeanquirit*, Stephen Heller; *Diamond* or *Wedel*, Zuccalmaglio; *Chiara, Chiarina* or *Zilia*, Clara Wieck; *Jonathan*, probably Schunke. All these characters Schumann introduced at will in the imaginary conversations which he wrote for the *Zeitschrift*. [Tr.]

able. For who will guarantee me against unforeseen changes and disturbances? Did I not say I could only promise regular assistance for two years at most, which does not necessarily imply complete severance at the end of that period? Two years would be long enough for me to learn something of business routine, to gain strength and clearness, without pedantry, in my views on art, and that without endangering my enjoyment of art for its own sake. But I confess I should like your words modified somewhat. Let us work in concert, so that if one sleeps the other is up and doing; if one draws in his horns, the other thrusts his out.

I claim your indulgence for my outspokenness, but, indeed, if our structure begins to shake in these early days of its foundation, the subsequent collapse is easy to foresee. If so complicated an undertaking is to be carried through at all, its promoters must give each other mutual and unconditional support. If your own support is conditional, as your letter of yesterday would seem to indicate, the fulfilment of the scheme must necessarily suffer.

I am not so foolish as to suppose that there is anything new to you in this letter, but I think you will hardly refuse my request to-day for an explanation of your attitude.

35.

To Franz Otto.

LEIPZIG, *August* 9, 1833.

DEAR OLD FRANZ OTTO,

What a tale I could unfold to you of sorrow and joy, lordly castles in the air, dreams of immortality and tears—of many things, in short! Your own unpleasant experiences do not seem to me so serious as your inability to derive pleasure and benefit from your stay. Well, you must now drink yourself strong again on German thought and the blood of the German eagle. Believe me, the home-sickness which Germans suffer abroad is not merely physical.

You must accept this letter, my dear fellow, as the beginning of a really connected correspondence, but for to-day I must be brief. May these lines herald a brighter future for music! We want a Hermann, with his Lessing under his arm, to make a way through the rabble. Do not flee the battle, but fight with us. Wieck has probably told you of the advent of a new musical periodical, which is to champion the cause of poetry by relentlessly attacking her present detractors. Your warm championship of truth and goodness, which I have long known and steadily recognized, induces me, in spite of my incomplete knowledge of your ideas, to ask you to put your hand to this work. You are already helping indirectly by your writings. But that is not enough. Direct criticism must step in to ensure the victory.

For the present, be as amusing as possible, and write English letters to brighten our first numbers, which are to make their trial appearance in October. So, my dear fellow, I hope you will find nothing more pressing to do, after reading these lines, than to sit down and mend a pen for these said English letters. I need not, of course, impress upon you how much depends on the first numbers, which, without promising too much, ought to make the public realize that a perceptible gap has been filled. If you do not care about making an elaborate setting for your ideas, leave all that to me; the original product shall shimmer through. As you are writing from a distance, the letter form is the liveliest and the most natural. You might address some imaginary person—a mistress, Vult Harnisch, Peter Schoppe.[1] However, I leave all that to your intelligence. The importance of the matter and old friendly feeling will urge you to let me know without delay whether the editorial staff may count upon the English letter for the first number. If there are any profits, and you go on writing, they hope to be able to promise you a decent salary. . . .

36.

To his Mother.

LEIPZIG, *November* 27, 1833.

. . . Not a word of these past weeks.[2] I was little better than a statue, feeling neither cold nor

[1] Characters in Jean Paul.

[2] Refers to the death of his brother Julius, on November 18, and of his sister-in-law, Rosalie, in October.

heat, until, with strenuous work, some life came into me again. I am still so nervous and timid that I cannot sleep alone; but I have found a thoroughly good-natured companion, and the very deficiencies of his education provide stimulus and distraction. Do you know, I had not the courage to travel to Zwickau alone for fear something might happen to me! Violent congestion, inexpressible terror, failure of breath, momentary unconsciousness—these overtake me in quick succession, though I am better than I was. If you had any notion of the lethargy into which melancholia has brought me you would forgive my not writing. One word more. Are you aware that a certain R. S. thinks of you hourly? Write to him, please, very soon. Farewell! Deep down in my heart lies something I would not lose at any price: the belief that there are some good people left—and a God. Am I not to be envied?

37.

To his Mother.

LEIPZIG, *January* 4, 1834.

I have only to-day read your letter. When I received it a week ago, and guessed the gloom of the whole from the first words, I had not the strength to read it through. As the mere thought of the troubles of others is so annihilating as to deprive me of all power of action, please spare me disturbing news, or I must give up your letters. Most particularly I beg you not to allude, either in speech or writing, to Julius and Rosalie. I did not know what pain was. Now it has come; and instead of my crushing it, it has crushed me a thousandfold. But in spite of this I have for some days felt fresher and better than for a long time past. Perhaps more cheerful ideas will gradually return, and then I will be so kind to everybody, as kind as they now are to me. You will find that hard to believe. But you are mistaken if you think that I am drawing more and more into myself. Any kindly word makes me happy; I should like to thank every one who addresses a word to me. I live quite simply. I have given up drinking any spirits, and walk a great deal every day with my good friend Ludwig Schunke, of whom you will have read. I have also worked better than for weeks past. Do not miss the *Davidsbündler* in the *Comet*. They are mine, and are making quite a sensation.

You ask if I have enough money. I must confess—no. The interest I draw and my earnings only amount for the present to 400 to 500 talers, and, unfortunately, I have never done with less than 600. But, believe me, these cares are inconsiderable compared with life's sufferings. Were they healed, happiness and energy would return and soon disperse the lighter troubles. Of this I am confident, and so must you be. The cloud-spots we think we see in the starlit sky are really radiant suns, indistinguishable to our weak sight. Indeed, I realize the sadness of your solitude.

Will you not go to Eduard or Karl? You owe your children, who love you so dearly, the longest possible life, which they in their turn will do their utmost to brighten. I have wished so often and so ardently that you would come to Leipzig for a time, and in now asking you I have not failed to consider how little compensation I can offer for the many precious things you would leave behind. But I should be trying to atone for a fault for which I often reproach myself. I do not act with sufficient consideration or gratitude towards you. I know, too, how hard it is for elderly people to reconcile themselves to entirely new circumstances, and how endlessly I should reproach myself if you were disappointed in the new circle. Think over all this, and let me know your opinion. I will not try to say how much pleasure it would give me if you agree to my honestly well-meant proposal. . . .

38.

To his Mother.

LEIPZIG, *July* 2, 1834.

I am not dead, or it would certainly have been in our paper, which must, on the contrary, often have conveyed to you signs that I am working hard and enjoying life. This two months' interval has had its gay and its sad side, and some of its events may even influence my whole future. I wish I could sit facing you, confide everything, question you, speak to you. On the gay side I place first of all my new sphere, my pleasure in the work, and in its effect on the public, with the recognition and praise of my efforts from outsiders. Then, too, the work brings me closer relationships, the friendship and esteem of good and true men on every side, and an existence divided between physical and mental enjoyment.

As for composing, it naturally proceeds more leisurely now, but you may see in the accompanying piece (a toccata) a proof of my uninterrupted efforts. You will hardly find anyone to play it in Zwickau. Just now I have to devote my whole energy to the paper. The others are not to be depended on. Wieck is constantly on tour; Knorr ill; Schunke has not much idea of wielding the pen; and who is left? Yet the paper is so extraordinarily successful that I go on working hard, but with satisfaction. Up to now three hundred orders have been received. In short, we are not stagnating.

Added to this, two glorious women have entered our circle. I told you before of Emilia, the sixteen-year-old daughter of the American consul, List—an English girl through and through, with bright, shining eyes, dark hair, and a firm step, full of spirit, dignity and life. The other is Ernestine, daughter of a rich Bohemian, Baron von Fricken—her mother was a Gräfin Zettwitz—a wonderfully pure, child-like character, delicate and thoughtful. She is really devoted to me, and cares for everything artistic. She is remarkably musical—everything, in a word, that I might wish my wife to be. A whisper in my dearest mother's ear—if the future asked me whom I would choose, I would answer with decision, 'This one.' But how far off that is, and how readily do I give up the prospect of a closer tie, however light it might be! Does my frankness displease you? No, or I myself should. Clara is in Dresden, and her genius continues to develop. The letters she writes—some to me—are remarkably clever. . . .

39.

To Ernestine von Fricken.[1]

LEIPZIG, *July* 28, 1834.

If I might say what I would, I should begin by thanking the good genius who permitted me to make your acquaintance, my dear young lady, and utilized the happy occasion at our dear Wieck's[2] to bring us into an outwardly closer relationship. I say 'outwardly,' for I am too modest to think that the belief in an inner, earlier artistic relation could give you pleasure. However that may be, I shall never be able to repay that good genius for a revelation of life deeper than any before, and for my admission to that circle of splendid men and

[1] Ernestine von Fricken, an illegitimate daughter of Captain (Freiherr) von Fricken, was born on September 7, 1816, and was formally adopted in 1834. Her silence on this matter may have cast the first shadow on her relations with Schumann. In 1838 she married, and was left a widow in the following year. She died in 1844. In spite of the breaking off of her engagement, she remained a true friend to Robert and Clara. Schumann dedicated his Chamisso songs (Op. 31) to her.

[2] They had stood sponsors to Wieck's daughter Cäcilie.

women to whom you have so permanently endeared yourself.

If ever I wished time would stand still, it is at this moment; and if ever I closed a letter with heartfelt devotion, it is this one.

40.

To Frau Henrietta Voigt.[1]

Undated [*Summer*, 1834].

DEAR LADY,

My behaviour—I don't know if that is the right word—I mean the way in which I have alternately accepted and rejected your manifold expression of interest in my unworthy self—is such a tangle of magnetic attraction and repulsion that I am anxious to justify my position in some particulars. And yet there is such confusion in the constellations. My life is so variegated that I must owe you an explanation until the conditions become clearer and calmer. I say this to you, dear friend, and to you alone; and if I might believe that you cared for this confession and the assurance of the deepest sympathy in all your affairs, it would be a comfort to me, though no excuse, for my way of showing sympathy seems to contradict itself. I beg you will be lenient in any case, if you still can. I am treasuring your last

[1] Schumann's friend Schunke had introduced him to Henrietta Voigt (*née* Kuntze), 1809-1839, the cultured wife of a Leipzig merchant. She was the confidante in his relations with Ernestine von Fricken.

letter. I have read it repeatedly, and have rejoiced inwardly in the lecture I shall some day read you on it. I only wish Eusebius, whose promise, or rather duty, struck him as he read your lines, might be depended on to finish the essay he had begun upon Berger, to whom your reflections would be equally applicable.

When Florestan read through the letter, he happened on a clever anagram. Where you wrote, 'Rochlitz,[1] who for so many years has stood faithfully by every *strebenden* (striving) artist,' etc., Florestan read, 'every *sterbenden* (dying) artist.' The description, I thought, applied to R., as the loving father who has closed the eyes of so many great people, and spoken over their graves. Florestan added that it reminded him of Lafayette watching a nation at its last gasp, and standing sentinel over the corpse. 'But where are you flying off to, Florestan?' I asked. 'This will bring us to the butterfly metaphor, for we love to imagine a Psyche rising from the crumbling dust.' I could give you more of this, but that Jean Paul would do it better. When you have a spare moment do, please, read the last[2] chapter of *Flegeljahre*, where you will find it all written down in black and white, down to the giant's boot, in F sharp minor. The close of the *Flegeljahre* always affects me in this

[1] Johann Friedrich Rochlitz (1769-1842), a well-known novelist and writer on music, and the first editor of the *Allgemeine musikalische Zeitung*.

[2] The last but one.

way. The piece is indeed over, but the curtain does not fall. I should like to mention, too, that I fitted the words to the music, and not *vice versa*, else were it a 'mad beginning.' Only the last number—by a freak of fortune similar to the first—was inspired by Jean Paul. One more question: Do not the *Papillons* explain themselves? It interests me to know.

Give these few lines, which are but a feeble reflection of all that I could say to you, the kind reception I can only wish they deserved.

R. S.

41.

To Captain von Fricken,[1] *Asch.*

[Zwickau], *November* 20, 1834.

May the hand that opens this letter be stronger than the one that seals it! Let my health account for my long silence—no great loss, indeed—and also for my flight to my native place, from which, my dear sir, I write you this letter. If Faust's cloak were mine I should certainly use it for a visit to your peaceful Asch, which I should, perhaps, find lighted for the evening. I should peep into your own room to see if you were keeping well, so you will know who it is if you see a flying figure. But imagination has its Faust-cloak, as I know only too well.

[1] Captain Ignaz Ferdinand, Freiherr von Fricken, father of Schumann's fiancée, Ernestine, was musical, and even composed a little. He, too, remained friends with Schumann.

Another thing that helped to drive me from Leipzig[1] was Schunke's illness; its stealthy advance terrifies me. It means the death of a fine man. Frau von Fricken would wish to close the eyes of a friend such as he. I have hardly got the better of my own illness, a very depressing form of melancholia. The word is easily written, but the thing itself is sometimes beyond human endurance. Forgive me if I complain of a matter of little interest to you. You will perhaps have more indulgence for a silence which it is seldom possible to break under the circumstances. Events took the course I predicted at Leipzig. I felt quite lost, for Schunke was confined to his room, and Wieck had gone north with Clara; so I came away, too, since those who were left were not likely to compensate for that lovely dream of spring. . . . I am glad you have solved my riddle,[2] though it was indeed no Œdipus puzzle. I had to laugh when I noticed next day that I had misspelt the name, and written 'Ashc.' I had played it for weeks without noticing the error, although it only took me a minute to compose.

I will spare myself a detailed reply until I send

[1] He had gone home on account of his health. [Tr.]

[2] Schumann, who was fond of such devices, had written a composition on the name 'Asch,' the Fricken estate. It so happened that the four letters tallied with the only 'musical' letters in 'Schumann,' S, C, H, A. (In German musical notation S (es) stands for E flat, As for A flat, and H for B natural. The piece referred to is probably the *Carnaval*, Op. 9, in which Schumann rings the changes on these notes.) [Tr.]

the Allegro,[1] which will follow shortly. One phrase in your letter haunts me, where you say that your imagination lies buried in the Bay of Naples. Don't forget that the sea has its pearls, and that you have been compensated by the gods with a gift which you would hardly exchange for what you have lost. I am importunate enough to ask to be remembered to this 'gift of the gods,' though my last greeting remained unacknowledged.

42.

To the Advocate Dr. Töpken,[2] Bremen.

LEIPZIG, *February* 6, 1835.

. . . But why do you leave me so long without a letter? In case you persist too long in your silence, I threaten to announce in one of the coming numbers that 'Herr T. Töpken, Doktor, our Bremen correspondent, died on. . . .' I assure you, all the subscribers are asking what has become of the Bremen correspondent. If good historical material is so scarce, you can always fill up with fine critical remarks. You know me well enough to be aware how little I care about artists, and how much about art. I mean that your copy can be as little personal as you like if gossip is lacking. But as I have heard nothing but good of your concerts, you should be the more inspired to write inspiringly, especially as you must have a side-

[1] Op. 8, dedicated to Ernestine von Fricken.

[2] Theodor Töpken, Dr. jur. (1807-1880), a friend of Schumann's from the Heidelberg days.

interest in them. So, my dear good fellow, I count on hearing from you soon.

I am now sole editor and proprietor. That is, I must put money into it for two years more, after which I hope for some return. How do you like the first numbers? In the last quarter of last year there was not enough solid opinion and finished criticism. But there are to be many improvements now. You may count upon that, and recommend the paper wherever you can, always provided that it does not offend your convictions.

. . . You know about Schunke?[1] I am now at work on his obituary. Your messages to him stared at me so pale and dumb from the paper. As man, as artist, and as friend, he had no equal. The *Davidsbündler* will tell you more of him. . . . How does my toccata displease you in its new form? I compose diligently, in spite of my editorial work. Have you the Allegro? It has little but good intention to recommend it. I wrote it four years ago, after my return from Heidelberg.

You would deserve better letters if you answered them sooner. In conclusion, here is an old maxim from Jean Paul: 'There is no better way of answering a letter than immediately on receiving it.' If nothing arrives by the 28th of February, I carry out my threat.

[1] Ludwig Schunke (1810-1834), a musician of great talent. He was one of Schumann's intimates, but their acquaintance lasted only one year. Schunke died of consumption on December 7, 1834.

43.

To his Sister-in-law, Theresa Schumann.

LEIPZIG, *April* 1, 1836.

I, too, have thought so much about you during the past weeks that it has seemed sometimes as though I might touch you by stretching out my hand. To know that you care for me gives me a feeling of shelter, of safety, of inexpressible happiness. That is because you have a great heart, and can give support, comfort and help.

Only the most favourable prospects would induce me to leave this place. Eduard can only have been joking about Vienna; he must be dreaming. In the first place, it is the haziest of plans, and could not be carried out before Christmas. Just think what I leave behind! First and foremost, there is my home, to which, I pray, I may never be cold or indifferent; then my family, and you yourself, who are within an hour's journey; Leipzig itself, with its gay, stirring life; then Clara; Mendelssohn, who is coming back next winter; and a hundred other considerations. If the change could really *fix* my future, I should not hesitate one second; but I will undertake nothing rashly and without guarantees. I should never be able to recover lost ground. So you may count on having me for another year, and I you—a year which shall be turned to the happiest use for both.

As regards the rest of my existence you would

really be pleased with me. With my usual liking for the extraordinary, I am now one of the slightest smokers and 'Bavarians,' though I was once the most hardened offender. Four cigars a day, and for the last two months no beer at all. As a result everything goes like clockwork, and I am really proud of myself. You need not praise me, you see, for I do it sufficiently on my own account.

Mendelssohn[1] . . . is a god among men, and you ought to know him. David,[2] the leader of the orchestra, is another of my associates; also a certain Dr. Schlemmer,[3] the companion of young Rothschild; and Rothschild himself. You will find these three in Leipzig when you come. The doctor will be quite one of your sort—a man of the world, every inch of him. Dr. Reuter[4] and Ulex[5] are, of course, friends of old standing. We will talk about Wieck and Clara when we meet. My position with them is critical, and I am not yet sufficiently collected

[1] Schumann always cherished the warmest admiration for Mendelssohn (1809-1847), who possessed the qualities which he himself lacked: mastery of form, clearness of expression, and ability in practical life. It is now generally admitted that Schumann's nature was richer and intenser. Outwardly, Mendelssohn treated Schumann with affection and respect, but he never really appreciated the romanticist.

[2] Ferdinand David (1810-1873), the famous violinist, leader of the Gewandhaus Orchestra at Leipzig, was one of Schumann's genuine admirers.

[3] Friedrich Schlemmer, Dr. jur., came from Frankfurt.

[4] M. E. Reuter (1802-1853), a doctor at Leipzig.

[5] Wilhelm Ulex, a music-teacher; died at Hamburg, 1858.

or clear to see my way. But as things stand, I either never speak to her again or I make her my very own. You shall learn all when you come, and will do your best for me. . . .

44.

To Theresa Schumann.

L(EIPZIG), *November* 15, 1836.

How often I see you in your cosy window-seat, your head resting on your hand, while you hum a song and wonder whether a certain 'Robert' is worth all the affection that is showered upon him! I was prevented from coming or writing by a succession of visits from Chopin,[1] Lipinski,[2] Mendelssohn, Mme. Carl,[3] Ludwig Berger,[4] and by a hundred other matters. How I should like to bring all these to you if you were here! You should see and make the acquaintance of people very different from the Zwickauites. There is a young fellow here now—Stamaty[5]—who dropped on me from the clouds; he is a clever, extremely handsome, well-bred, and thoroughly good creature. He was born in Rome of Greek parents, brought

[1] Schumann was among the pioneers of Chopin's music in Germany.

[2] Karl Lipinski (1790-1861), 'first violin' at Leipzig.

[3] Henriette Carl (1815-1896), a singer who held an appointment at the Prussian Court.

[4] Ludwig Berger (1777-1839), of Berlin, a well-known composer for the pianoforte. He taught Mendelssohn.

[5] Camille Stamaty (1811-1870), a well-known pianist, composer and teacher. Saint-Saëns is one of his pupils.

up in Paris, and is now here to finish his studies with Mendelssohn. You would like him very much. We had actually made up our minds to come to Zwickau for the musical festival; the idea was dropped. Anyway, he will stay here until the spring, so you will see him in the fair-time, unless we come to see you in the interval. He is still very weak in German, which is good for my French. Then there is a young Englishman, William Bennett,[1] among our daily intimates—an Englishman through and through. He is a splendid artist, a poetic, noble nature. Perhaps I shall bring him too. Mendelssohn is engaged, and this absorbing interest makes him kinder and greater than ever. Hardly a day passes without his producing at least one or two ideas worthy of a golden setting. His fiancée is Cecilia Jeanrenaud, daughter of a pastor of the Reformed Church, and cousin to Dr. Schlemmer. He is going to Frankfurt at Christmas to see her, and will take me—perhaps. Dr. Schlemmer has at length received a Hessian Order, which he will bear with credit; I have long foreseen that he would be decorated before he died. He is with Rothschild at Heidelberg. David is to be married one of these days, but sticks to his post in spite of his wife's dowry of 100,000 talers. Besides these, my

[1] Schumann was to the end a champion of William Sterndale Bennett (1816-1875). Even Clara's arguments failed to bring him to a more reasonable estimation of the composer who so closely resembled Mendelssohn. Bennett certainly rendered valuable service to the cause of music in England.

dining companions include Franck, a young man from Breslau—young, talented, and very rich; also young Goethe,[1] the old man's grandchild, whose character is as yet undeveloped. . . .

For no eyes but yours!

C[lara] loves me as much as ever, but I have quite given up hope. I often go to the Voigts. The old round! . . .

45.

To A. von Zuccalmaglio.[2]

LEIPZIG, *January* 31, 1837.

MY VERY DEAR SIR,

First let me tell you that a few days ago I handed Mr. Mendelssohn, with whom I dine regularly, your essay, *Erste Töne*, to read. I watched from a distance to see how he would screw up his face when he came to that passage at the end, which, I confess, brought the tears to my eyes. He read it attentively, betraying, by the expression of his noble, unforgettable face, his increasing approval. Then came the particular passage. You should have seen him! 'Ah! what's this? It is really too much; this gives me real pleasure. One gets praised in all sorts of ways, but this comes straight from the heart,' etc. You should have seen and heard him! 'Many, many

[1] Walther von Goethe (1817-1885), to whom Schumann dedicated the *Davidsbündlertänze*.

[2] Anton Wilhelm Florentin Zuccalmaglio (1803-1869), one of the best contributors to Schumann's paper.

thanks to the writer!' And so he went on; and then we plunged into champagne.

But really I have been saying to myself for a long time that no one has ever written about music like Wedel.[1] Every turn of thought is so artistic, every cadence so musical. It is like reading in Mendelssohn's face, which is so mobile as to reflect his own thoughts and his surroundings as well. But enough.

Do you know his *Saint Paul*, which is a chain of beautiful thoughts. He is actually the first to give the graces a place in church music, and they really should not be forgotten, although up till now the ubiquitous fugue has barred the way. Do read *Saint Paul*, and the sooner the better. In spite of what people say, there is no trace of Händel or Bach in it beyond what is common to all church music. If I could but see you and talk to you in the summer! I am sorry to say that you will probably not find Mendelssohn here, as he is to spend the summer with his fiancée in Frankfurt. His engagement makes a perfect child of him.

Have you any smaller poems, suitable for musical composition, for the paper? I cannot help you with your tragedy. At the mere mention of the word 'tragedy,' Barth[2] looked me up and down. But if you will arrange your 'Wedeliana,' I can, I hope, help you there. . . .

[1] Zuccalmaglio's pen-name.

[2] The publisher, J. A. Barth.

46.

To A. von Zuccalmaglio.

LEIPZIG, *May* 18, 1837.

. . . Mendelssohn possesses the only copy of Bach's D minor concerto, but as soon as he comes back from the Rhine—at the end of September—I will have a copy made for you, likewise one for myself, for I have always thought it one of the most admirable productions ever written.

I am really sorry you are not coming, as there are various things I wanted to talk over with you, which I have no leisure to write. First, I have been thinking for some time of giving life to the *Davidsbündler;* that is, of uniting through the bond of the pen like-minded people, whether they are musicians by profession or not. If academies with ignoramuses of presidents at their head elect their members, why should not we juniors elect each other? I am also simmering with another idea which might easily be combined with the first, but is of more general importance. It is the establishment of an agency for publishing the works of all composers who conform to its rules, its object being to transfer to the composers the liberal profits which now go to the publishers. The only essential is a qualified agent to carry on the business. The composers would have to give security for the expenses of setting up their works, and would receive, say, half-yearly accounts of the sales and the distribution of the surplus after deducting expenses. This much for the present! Think the matter over seriously, as it might be made a great benefit to all artists. Think it over, please, and write to me. . . .

47.

To J. Moscheles, Flottbeck, near Hamburg.

LEIPZIG, *August* 23, 1837.

I am again sending you, my very dear Sir, two compositions, different enough. The *Maskentanz*[1] will be child's play to you. I need hardly tell you, perhaps, that the arrangement of the whole and the inscriptions over the separate pieces were added after the music was written. The *Studies*[2] I can present to you with more confidence. Some of them I still like—they are nearly three years old. You know what your opinion means to me. Send me a line or two, just for myself.

I am like a child looking forward to Christmas at the prospect of seeing your *Studies*. I still fail to find any announcement of the Concerto *pathétique*. And now, just one favour. It concerns art as well as my own interest. I have succeeded in persuading the publishers of my paper to publish some considerable composition as a quarterly supplement. I hope to start many nice ideas in this way. It will make quite a stir among musicians. For instance, I mean to have the words of songs written out, and the most interesting printed side by side in one number, with probably

[1] The *Carnaval*. [2] The *Symphonic Studies*.

a bad one thrown in to make it easier for the critic to point his moral, and for the reader to follow him music in hand. Particular attention will be devoted to the manuscripts of unknown musicians of genuine talent. They will see themselves famous all at once, for the paper has five hundred readers, to whom the compositions will be sent gratis. From time to time the supplement will consist of old pieces which only exist in manuscript, such as the Scarlatti fugues, or even a whole Bach concerto in the full score. Then I should like to join with my friends in a cycle of smaller compositions. One would begin; the next, after seeing what had been written, would add something, and so on, the idea being to give to the whole the unity which is so conspicuously absent from the ordinary album. In short, I am brimful of ideas.

My immediate attention, however, is given to preparing four Studies of different masters, to form the New Year's number for 1838. Since I am so much interested in all that concerns you, my very dear Sir, I naturally wondered whether you would spare us one of your *Études* from your second volume for our paper, before Kistner publishes them. A name like yours would immediately inspire confidence, and our first step would be a triumph. Chopin has promised me one too, and I have one by A. Henselt,[1] the most brilliant of our younger composers—you will be delighted with

[1] Adolf Henselt (1814-1889), pianist and composer, wrote many delightful pianoforte pieces and studies.

him. As to the fourth, I am still hesitating whether I should approach Mendelssohn or some one else about it.

48.

To Simonin de Sire, Dinant, Belgium.[1]

LEIPZIG, *February* 8, 1838.

SIR,

The first thing I did on receiving your letter was to look up Dinant on the map, with the idea of delivering my thanks for your kindness in person, if the place were not too far from Saxony. But even if I cannot fix a time for a meeting, tied as I am to the staff of a paper, I can spend many a free hour pleasurably and profitably in communing with a friend of art such as every line of your letter shows you to be. Rest assured that I shall do my part. Living as I do in a busy art centre, I can send you varied information which would otherwise reach you by roundabout ways, or perhaps, by ill chance, not at all. In a word, I will visit you sometimes as a faithful Mercury from the heaven of music. Our new paper will certainly give you the speediest and fullest account of everything, and the severity and high aim of its criticism should meet with your particular approval. You will easily believe that everything relating to the pianoforte is given a certain preference. Need I apologize for writing

[1] Simonin de Sire (1800-1872), a landowner of Dinant, Belgium, one of Schumann's earliest and most ardent admirers outside Germany.

in German? Really, my French will not do for anything beyond Herz and Hünten.[1] Beethoven demands my mother-tongue. But I hope this will not lower me in your esteem. With regard to my composition, I can hardly tell you how much good your sympathy does me. We welcome sympathy from any quarter, but how much more heartily from the genuine art-lover, who is, indeed, rare as the genuine artist himself! Then, too, I feel that my path is fairly solitary; no acclaiming crowd inspires me to fresh effort, but I keep my eyes fixed on my great examples, Bach and Beethoven, whose far-off images give unfailing help and encouragement. Indeed, I find few who understand me, but I have my compensation in the affection of three people—Liszt,[2] Clara Wieck, and now yourself. You will, I think, find more refinement and artistic merit in some of my other compositions than in the small pieces with which you are acquainted. I should like to draw your attention particularly to the sonatas 'Florestan' and 'Eusebius,' the two books of *Fantasiestücke* and the *Concert sans orchestre*.

[1] Herz (1803-1888) and Hünten (1793-1878), two successful writers of light music, to whom Schumann offered strong opposition on account of their baneful influence on the public taste.

[2] We shall find frequent proof of Schumann's admiration for Liszt and Liszt's esteem for Schumann. But Schumann's quiet, reserved temperament led him to regard Liszt's methods with misgivings, which time and a keener insight into musical life only served to strengthen. Liszt remained faithful to his admiration for Schumann as man and as artist.

The human heart is often a strange spectacle in which sorrow and joy are strangely blended. You have still to expect my best work; for I am conscious of a certain inward strength, and can even go so far as to say that I believe the science of sound, considered as the soul's speech, to be still in its infancy. May my good genius inspire me, and bring this undeveloped science to maturity.

I have sent a list of my complete works to Messrs. Breitkopf and Härtel, who will supply you with everything. I miss from your library, of which you kindly sent me some account, the names of Franz Schubert, Mendelssohn, Bennett, Adolf Henselt, and Clara Wieck. Perhaps you would like me to send you the names of their principal works? The first three contain more that is of interest to the musician than the pianist, it is true, but the two last named have reached the highest level in the art of playing, the level of Chopin and Liszt.

I am exceedingly interested in your discovery. I have seriously thought over similar matters myself, as no single one of the existing pianoforte schools satisfies me. Be sure you write to me about it. I should also be glad to hear any details of the musical life in your neighbourhood, about which we hear so little.

I could write much more, my dear sir, but will content myself for to-day with closing this letter with a greeting which, coming from the heart of an artist, will, I hope, strike an answering chord in your own!

49.

To Eduard and Karl Schumann.

LEIPZIG, *March* 19, 1838.

MY DEAREST BROTHERS EDUARD AND KARL,

I can write to you to-day with a lighter heart than for this long time past. You will know what that means. I have reason to know that 'Papa' will gradually melt, and that one of the loveliest maidens the world ever brought forth will in time be my own. It is sad, on the other hand, that I may have to be separated from you for a long time. A large town is the only place for an artist of her calibre, and I, too, should like to change my sphere. We shall, therefore, probably move to Vienna. My future holds the fairest prospects, my paper goes with me; Clara has a great name there, and can earn considerable sums by playing; I myself am not unknown; and Clara writes that there would be no difficulty about getting an appointment for her as professor at the Vienna Conservatoire, thanks to the Empress's personal liking for her. On reflection you will have to admit that everything favours the plan. If all goes smoothly—that is, if Friese[1] will release me from my contract a year earlier (I am really bound till the end of 1840)—if I can, as I don't doubt, find a publisher in Vienna, and if I can obtain a license from the Government there for my paper, which cannot be refused me, the old man

[1] Robert Friese (1805-1848) published Schumann's paper.

will give his consent. At Christmas, 1839, therefore, I shall probably go straight to Vienna, set up house, and fetch my dear girl at Easter. Pray that Heaven may bless the enterprise. Of myself I can only say that I cannot look forward to this splendid prospect for sheer ecstasy.

But there is a prosaic side to all the beautiful things in life, and from this you have to suffer. But you will see the importance of this matter, and must surely love your brother (of whom you are a little proud) too much to fail to assist him with your whole strength towards the desired goal.

So talk it over with my dear Theresa, and decide how you can pay off gradually some of your debt to me. The removal and the start in housekeeping will be expensive, and it would never do to appear before Wieck empty-handed. This is what I propose:

That you pay me every Easter, beginning from this year, 600 talers each besides the interest, or, if possible, more; but I will be satisfied with that. In this way you will pay off your debt in six or seven years without feeling it so much, and I shall not receive it in driblets, which always run through one's fingers. I should then have 2,400 talers in hand for the first part of the time in Vienna (1840). I can leave it untouched until then, as I shall have enough for ordinary purposes with the salary I receive from the paper, and the income from my compositions (the price of which steadily advances) is sufficiently assured. Remember that it concerns

8—2

the fate of the most glorious of girls, from whom I cannot be parted, who is also the greatest of artists. It concerns a connexion which will be the greatest adornment to our family, and a brilliant future which cannot fail to reflect favourably on yourselves. Later on I may, perhaps, be able to help you again, if you should be pressed; but for the present you will have to bestir yourselves to give me what I ask; you cannot think it anything but fair, and must on no account refuse compliance.

I ask you particularly to preserve a strict silence on all these matters; the old man must know nothing of our private correspondence, or he might cool off. Be equally discreet with every one about the idea of a move to Vienna, or you may spoil everything for me. I will say no more of my happiness in possessing a girl with whom I have grown to be one through art, intellectual affinities, the regular intercourse of years, and the deepest and holiest affection. My whole life is one joyous activity.

I hope you will sympathize in my happiness, and be ever the affectionate brothers you have always been.

50.

To Theresa Schumann.

LEIPZIG, *March* 25, 1838.

If you had read my last letter to Clara, you would have understood why it is so hard for me to leave here. But Providence has guided the course of events, and will continue to do so. I hope you mean to come with us to Vienna for the wedding, and then we can spend together a few weeks which will serve for a year or more of happy recollections. After all, the degree of distance does not matter much. Do we ever see one another oftener than once a year as it is? I may surely still count on a yearly visit to you, especially as Clara's parents remain in Leipzig for the present. Courage, then, and we can write what we have not the opportunity of saying. Clara has often wished to write to you herself. I told her she might call you sister, to which she replied: 'I should indeed like to call her sister, but there is still one little word to add to sister, the same little word that has brought us so close together and made us so happy.' But she has really not had time to write, scarcely even to me, so you must not be angry with her. She will probably spend a few hours with you, however, on her return from Munich. I will let you know the exact date later, and you will give the noble girl the reception she deserves at your hands for my sake. I cannot tell you, Theresa, what a wonderful creature she is, what wonderful qualities she has, and how unworthy I am of her. But I mean to make her happy. Spare me any more words, for my emotion is too great. But call her 'sister' when you see her, and think of me as you do so.

Now for one more important affair in which I want your advice and assistance. Clara has been raised to rather a high rank by her appointment as Court pianist. I have, of course, also my title, but it is not equal to hers. For myself I am content to die an artist, and recognize no superior but art; but on account of her parents I should like to have my share of honours. You know Hartenstein well; will you write to him or to Ida to this effect:

That I (do as you like and as you think best about giving my name) am engaged to a girl of good social standing with the consent of her parents, to whom it would certainly be a gratification if I could write 'Doctor' before my name. The honour would hasten matters. Now, I should like to find out through Hartenstein's[1] kindness if there would be much fuss about obtaining the degree from the faculty of philosophy. I should not have much time to give to it, as I am so pressed with all sorts of professional work. Ask him to tell you how I could set about it. I only want it for the sake of the title, and should then be leaving Leipzig for good. There is no great hurry, in any case, but once I had his opinion I could go into it further myself. Then you might ask him if the university of Leipzig will not create doctors of music. Lastly, I beg him and Ida to preserve strict silence about it, as it is to be a surprise. You women can do anything, so do whisper to Ida

[1] Dr. Gustav Hartenstein (1808-1890), professor of philosophy at Leipzig. His wife came from Gera, and was thus acquainted with Schumann's sister-in-law, Theresa.

that she might remember an old acquaintance. I want you to take the matter to heart. Do what you can, and write soon. . . .

51.

To J. Fischhof.[1]

LEIPZIG, *August* 5, 1838.

MY DEAR FRIEND,

I received your kind letter just as I was thinking of sitting down to write to you about a very important matter, as it happens, in which I need the advice of a tried friend like yourself. You must not be surprised if within a few months my double—that is, myself—comes knocking at your door, and announces that he is going to spend the next few years in Vienna, and perhaps settle there for good. . . . More when I see you; I cannot write it. It is settled that I must be in Vienna by October at the latest. And the paper? you will ask. Of course, I am not giving it up. Oswald Lorenz is looking after it from October to December, and from January onwards it is to be printed in Vienna, where I need your kind help. We must, of course, have a license for it, which is, I suppose, to be obtained from the censor's office under Count Sedlnitzky. I am convinced that they will not raise any great difficulties, as it is purely an art paper, and has from the first circulated in the Austrian States; but, knowing from hearsay how cautious

[1] Joseph Fischhof (1804-1857), had been professor of the pianoforte at the Vienna Conservatorium since 1833.

the authorities are, and how slowly such transactions are put through, I must set the matter in motion at once, and send in my request for permission to bring out the paper in Vienna immediately, if the first number of the new volume is to be distributed from Vienna in the middle of December. As I am entirely ignorant of the form and phrasing in which such a request should be couched for Austria, I beg you to come to the help of a poor artist who has had no experience of the administration and the censorship. I shall never forget any obligation to you in this matter.

Would you, then, please ask your lawyer to whom the request should be addressed, and how it should be worded? Perhaps you could ask him to draw up the actual petition by the aid of my sketch over the page, and send it on to me. I could then have a fair copy made, and perhaps send it to Sedlnitzky through our Ambassador, Prince Schönburg, to whom I have an introduction. Then, can you tell me whether the Viennese authorities will require information relative to my previous occupation, my financial position (my affairs are all in order), and so on, and if I ought to produce this with the petition? Lastly, whom do you recommend as agent for Friese? We have tried Haslinger and Diabelli, but neither of them responds as we should have liked. I should prefer a bookseller in any case, as I should then have nothing to fear from possible interference on the part of publishers. Friese is still to be the publisher; I am the proprietor. He really likes the idea of the change, as he only stands to gain by it. The paper would have on it the name of a Vienna firm, as well as his.

I should have to begin a fresh sheet were I to tell you all the beautiful things I expect from the future: how the journal is to enlarge its range, to increase its influence, and form a bond between north and south. You are the only man I know in Vienna who is intelligent, as well as thorough and modest. You will not be disappointed in me, or lose your friendly feeling for me? Do you not also look forward to much that is beautiful in the future, which will surely not deceive us?

I close my letter with unusual emotion, and with a grateful heart. Let me have your help, for my life's happiness depends partly on it; I am no longer alone. All this is for your eyes only. . . .

The petition to be turned into the proper legal hash:—the undersigned, a Saxon by birth, resident in Leipzig, musician, editor and proprietor of the new *Zeitschrift für Musik*, purposes, from love of his art and from business considerations, to exchange his present place of abode, Leipzig, for Vienna. The journal, which has always been devoted exclusively to musical matters, has had, since its beginning in 1834, the approval of the highest officials in the kingdom, and has been much read. He asks for permission to publish it in Vienna from January 1, 1839—that is, from the tenth volume—and will be happy to produce any necessary statements about his former circumstances. As he is prevented by business from coming to Vienna before the middle of October, he now sends in his petition with a request for consideration.

(All this with the proper professions of humility.)

* * * * *

I am better at composing, eh? Well, thanks once more for your kind letters. . . . We shall soon meet. I smoke a great many cigars, and am getting a fine colour. What is the rent of a decent flat for a year, on the first floor, if possible?—100 to 120 talers? Please help the stranger. Good-bye.

52.

To his Relatives in Zwickau.

VIENNA, *October* 10, 1838.

I am not calm enough at this moment to tell you all that has taken place with regard to myself and my circumstances since we parted. I had not been here two days before I received the most alarming news from Leipzig, which at once absorbed all my thoughts. The old ——, who has only been made more furious by our energetic action, has been storming at Clara again; but she opposes him quietly and firmly. What has happened since I do not know, but I fear much. My request to Clara to leave her father at once and live with you for a time may have arrived too late. If she should come, you will, I know, treat her as a sister.

I have not so far made much advance in my

undertaking. The city is so large that everything takes double time. I have met with a friendly reception from every one, including the minister of police, with whom I had an audience the day before yesterday. He told me that there was no objection to my being here, and that I should experience no difficulties once I had found an Austrian publisher for the paper. Should I fail to find one, there might be difficulties for me as a foreigner. I am anxious to take the first steps before I see him again, and propose to go to Haslinger to-day or to-morrow. You would hardly believe what petty cliques and sets there are here. To obtain a firm footing one needs a good deal of the wisdom of the serpent, of which, I fear, I have little. But courage! Our great hope lies in Frau von Cibbini,[1] who is all-powerful. Clara has written her a splendid letter and told her everything. But she will not be back before the 24th.

I am thirsting for news of you and Clara. It has been impossible to find a confidant in the short time, and consequently I am in a state of inward ferment. If my thoughts were not so much occupied, I might easily fall ill. I take a great pleasure in the really admirable performances at the opera, particularly in the chorus and orchestra, of which we in Leipzig have no notion. The ballet would

[1] Katharina Cibbini, *née* Kozeluch (1790-1858), lady-in-waiting to the Empress Maria Anna, was herself an excellent pianist and a composer.

amuse you, too. I have not yet been to the German theatre, which is acknowledged to be the first in Germany, or to the smaller variety theatres. . . .

Clara was absolutely worshipped here. Wherever I inquire they tell me so, and speak of her in the most affectionate terms. But, indeed, there can hardly be such another inspiring audience in the world; it is even too enthusiastic, for you hear more clapping than music in the theatre. It is all very gay, but it irritates me sometimes. Well, our affair must be settled within the next few weeks. If I cannot stay here I am firmly resolved to go to Paris or to London. I will not return to Leipzig. Of course, it all has to be thought out, and you need not fear that I shall act in undue haste. As soon as I have anything certain to tell you I will write. Please answer immediately. Best love to all.

53.

To Theresa Schumann.

VIENNA, *Wednesday, December* 18, 1838.

I could write you whole sheets and volumes, but have no time; so here is just a greeting for Christmas Eve. You will probably spend it as I shall, your head on your hand, thinking of old times. I shall be with you in thought, with Clara, and shall watch you deck your Christmas-tree. Yes, there will come a beautiful time when we three spend our Christmas together, sooner, perhaps, than we think. It is like a dream to think of you and the rest in Leipzig. I can well imagine how you feel sometimes. Clara has been in Dresden; she is very sorry she has so little opportunity of answering you, but you will forgive her. You know her whole nature is made up of love and devotion and gratitude. She makes me very happy in the midst of this material Viennese life. Do you know, Theresa, that if it depended on me, I would go back to Leipzig to-morrow. It is no such insignificant place as I thought it. Here people are as gossipy and provincial as in Zwickau. I have to be very careful as a public personage of some reputation; they spy on me at every corner. I am also inclined to doubt whether there is anything more in the so-called good nature of the Viennese than a smiling face. I have not had any bad experiences myself, but I hear extraordinary things from and about other people. As for artists, I have sought them in vain; by artists I mean not simply those who play one or two instruments passably, but good all-round people capable of understanding Shakespeare and Jean Paul. Well, the step is taken, as it had to be, though it is obvious the paper must lose by being published here. Once I have my wife, all that this affair has cost me in trouble and sleepless nights will be forgotten.

I could tell you much of my acquaintance with great people: of the Empress, whom I have seen and fallen in love with (she is a real Spaniard); of the Burg theatre, which is really excellent; of Thalberg, with whom I am on friendly terms; and of my paper, for which I have not yet received the desired license, so that it must continue to appear for another six months in Leipzig. Of myself I can say that I often feel well enough here, though oftener melancholy enough to shoot myself. Miss Novello[1] is engaged to one of my dearest friends, to my great delight. All these items should be dealt with at length, but the days fly so quickly. To think that I have been here twelve weeks to-day! The post-time, which is four o'clock here, has come round again, so I will only add the most important things. Clara goes to Paris in the beginning of January, and later to London probably, so that we shall be far enough apart. You know the reason, however; she wants to earn money, which we need badly. May Heaven keep watch over my dear, faithful girl! I may perhaps go to Salzburg for a month in the spring, possibly to Leipzig also, should it be necessary to talk over things connected with the paper with Gerold[2] and Friese. In any case, we shall live in Vienna for the first few years, unless difficulties are put in our way. I shall yet have to naturalize myself as an Austrian citizen. It is no hard matter to earn money here,

[1] Clara Novello (*b.* 1818), daughter of the well-known English publisher, was an excellent oratorio-singer. Schumann had known her at Leipzig. Her engagement to Schumann's friend, Dr. F. Weber, was broken off, and she married Count Gigliucci in 1843.

[2] Karl Gerold, a bookseller in Vienna.

for they need people with their wits about them. I am sure all will go well with us. Don't be afraid, dear Theresa. . . .

54.

To Simonin de Sire.

VIENNA, *March* 15, 1839.

It is a fortnight now since I received your treasured, long-looked-for letter, my very dear sir, but I have not had an hour in which to answer it as I should wish. I was beginning to think our acquaintance was a myth, and thought you had quite forgotten me. Your letter, however, is a charming proof to the contrary, and I thank you heartily for the uplifting, strengthening effect of your words. You will be surprised at my writing to you from Vienna. I have been here since October, on private business primarily, but secondarily for musical matters. I have not formed any deep attachments, but Vienna must always be a city of many and varied attractions and advantages to musicians. I have myself written some few things here, though not my best.

Since you inquire with such interest for my new compositions, the following completed works have been published: Op. 15, *Kinderszenen* (Breitkopf and Härtel); Op. 16, *Kreisleriana* (Haslinger, Vienna); and Op. 17, *Phantasie*, in three movements (Breitkopf and Härtel); and in four or five weeks' time, Mechetti of this city will publish:

Op. 18, *Arabeske;* Op. 19, *Blumenstück;* Op. 20, *Humoreske.* Of all these, *Kreisleriana* is my favourite. The title conveys nothing to any but Germans. Kreisler is one of E. T. A. Hoffmann's creations, an eccentric, wild, and witty conductor. You will like some of it. The inscriptions over my pieces always occur to me after I have finished composing the music. Neither does *Humoreske* convey anything in French. It is a pity that no good and apt words exist in the French language for those two most characteristic and deeply rooted of German conceptions, *Das Gemütliche* (*Schwärmerische*) and *Humor*, the latter of which is a happy combination of *Gemütlichkeit* and wit. But this bears out the whole character of the two nations. You know our great author Jean Paul? I have learnt more counterpoint from him than from my music-teacher. How I wish I could talk over all this with you some time, my dear sir, and hear your views. An evil fate has deprived me of the full use of my right hand, so that I am not able to play my compositions as I feel them. The trouble with my hand is that certain fingers have become so weak, probably through writing and playing too much at one time, that I can hardly use them. This has often depressed me, though Heaven from time to time sends me an inspiration which keeps me from thinking any more about it.

I am glad to hear about your compositions, and shall order them from Schott at once. There is nothing against your system of writing except that it is strange to the eye, and most people find it difficult enough to take in two staves at once. Hünten and Czerny[1] would be in despair if your system came in, as their own ideas barely fill one. Hearty thanks for your communication. I should like sometime to use the theme myself, particularly the first half, which has such a singing character.

You really must not neglect to publish your letters on the new tendencies in pianoforte music. The time is just ripe; something fresh will arise shortly, and lessen their effect. Schott would certainly be glad to publish the pamphlet, and I would be answerable for a good German translation. Among the older composers who have exercised great influence on modern music I would draw your attention to Franz Schubert, in the first place, and also to Prince Louis Ferdinand of Prussia,[2] two deeply poetical temperaments. You are, of course, acquainted with Schubert's songs; but I place at least as high his compositions for the pianoforte, especially those for four hands. Of younger men I can only name to you Stephan Heller[3] and

[1] Karl Czerny (1791-1857), the famous composer of educational pianoforte works.

[2] Prince Louis Ferdinand of Prussia (1772-1806), nephew of Frederick the Great, was killed in the battle of Saalfeld. His compositions show great talent, and are obviously influenced by Beethoven, whose greatness he was one of the first to recognize.

[3] Stephan Heller (1814-1888), a famous pianist and composer of great charm.

Ferdinand Hiller,[1] both capable exponents of the new ideas. Clara Wieck, who is at this moment in Paris, has had eight compositions published so far, all of which you should try to get. She is an admirable artist, and a still more admirable girl. Mendelssohn I consider the first musician of the day; I doff my hat to him as my superior. He plays with everything, especially with the grouping of the instruments in the orchestra, but with such ease, delicacy and art, with such mastery throughout. Bennett follows in his steps. The two of them are like angels at the pianoforte, as unaffected as children. Thalberg is only important as a virtuoso. He has, in my opinion, no invention except in technique. But he is in the first rank of virtuosi, whether as an interpreter of his own works or of those of other composers. . . .

55.

To A. von Zuccalmaglio.

LEIPZIG, *April* 27, 1839.

I think my respite from the journal has been beneficial to me, for it has regained the youthful beauty it had for me when we founded it. Indeed, there is more need than ever of hard work and endurance. Our Stuttgart quack-doctor[2] is begin-

[1] Ferdinand Hiller (1811-1885), is now almost forgotten as a composer. Schumann succeeded him as Director at Düsseldorf, but was, in this capacity, no substitute for Hiller, who did so much for music in the Rhine country.

[2] Gustav Schilling (1803-1881), first a theologian, then an only too prolific writer on music. His worthless character was

ning to give himself airs, and, arch-braggart as he is, without, to my mind, the faintest conception of music, he knows how to use words and titles, and we must direct our energies against him. How those old gentlemen, Spohr, Schneider, and the rest, can permit such a boasting ignoramus to lead them by the nose passes my comprehension. Perhaps he will make you a correspondent, as he has done me without my knowledge.

56.

To H. Dorn.

LEIPZIG, *September* 5, 1839.

MY VERY DEAR, KIND FRIEND,

Your long-expected letter reached me late enough, only ten or twelve days ago. It must have lain by for some time at Königsberg. I am sorry to have to do without your correspondence in the paper, though I see that is unavoidable. Indeed, I do not know how I can expect anything more from you after your many tokens of interest and sympathy, for which I can make you so small a return. Yet, when I study your handwriting more closely, the old time comes back, bringing with it the half-warning, half-smiling, familiar face of my teacher, and I understand how it is that I am asking another favour.

I should be very pleased if you could find room

afterwards revealed to Schumann, or, rather, to Clara, who had experience of him as a wolf in sheep's clothing. He was forced to escape to America. (*Cf.* Litzmann, *Clara Schumann*, i. 276-282, 286-289.)

for me in your gallery, for the world knows practically nothing of me. You know why I ask? We sometimes think we can do without this sort of thing, but in my heart of hearts I am inclined to agree with Jean Paul when he says that air and praise[1] are the only things man can and should absorb incessantly. But I am far from complaining, for I am really happy in my art, and have set a long term of work before me. Then, too, I have some one—Clara—at my side to encourage and uplift me. I might call her my fiancée, but it is a hateful story, for, you know, we have had to bring an action against her father, because, I being neither a fool nor a millionaire, he refuses his consent. We expect the permission before long from a court of law, in which case we may visit you in Riga. I am living on the edge of a volcano, as you may imagine, but I felt I could no longer leave Clara's old friend and mine in the dark now that the affair has become public. I count upon your sincere congratulations. My girl is one in a thousand; her nature is noble through and through.

Some traces of the battles I have had to fight on Clara's account may perhaps be discernible in my music, and you will not fail to comprehend them. The concerto, the sonata, the *Davidsbündler* dances, the *Kreisleriana*, and the *Novelettes*, may be said to have been almost entirely inspired by her. I have seldom met with anything so clumsy and commonplace as Rellstab's criticism of my

[1] In *Flegeljahre* the passage runs, 'Praise is the only air which,' etc.

Kinderszenen. He seems to think I call up in my imagination a screaming child, and fit the notes to it. It is just the other way about, but I will not deny that a vision of children's heads haunted me as I wrote. The inscriptions arose, of course, afterwards, and are really nothing more than tiny finger-posts to the interpretation and conception. But Rellstab, really, hardly goes beyond the A B C of music at times; chords are the only thing he understands. Then I am far from considering Klein[1] a great master. Berger was, in his small way, much more productive. Set my mind at rest with a few words on the subject, and tell me if I am right.

I do not know whether it is advisable to have anything in my paper about myself. Much would depend on the form it took; it should also be pointed out that Fink has the best reasons for not entering on any such topic. I leave all this, in any case, to your judgment. . . .

57.

To Ernst A. Becker.[2]

LEIPZIG, *December* 11, 1839.

. . . Dear Becker, I heard parts of Franz Schubert's symphony[3] at the rehearsal to-day, and it

[1] Bernhard Klein (1793-1832), in his time an esteemed composer of the Berlin school. Posterity endorses Schumann's low opinion of him.

[2] Ernst Adolf Becker (1798-1874), proved a true and self-sacrificing friend, particularly in Schumann's fight to win Clara. He was a government official, also an excellent pianist.

[3] The C major symphony, discovered by Schumann among the literary remains in the possession of Schubert's brother during his stay in Vienna.

realized all the ideals of my life. It is the greatest achievement in instrumental music since Beethoven, not excepting even Spohr and Mendelssohn. Do make a point of getting it for yourself at Freiberg. It is to be published very shortly by Breitkopf. It has made me tingle to be at work on a symphony, too, and I believe something will come of it, once I am happily married to Clara. . . .

58.

To Keferstein.[1]

LEIPZIG, *January* 31, 1840.

MY VERY DEAR SIR AND FRIEND,

Your kind letter with the interesting enclosure only reached me to-day. I have only had time to peep into the latter, but must write a few lines of thanks for the former without delay.

There is a long interval between this letter and my last, also much joy and sorrow from the point of view of art and life. In the editorial holidays the composer is to the fore; moreover, circumstances of the most exciting nature have made great demands on my time and strength. I must beg you, therefore, to excuse my long silence. May I confess that I have often doubted whether you take the same interest in the efforts of young artists as of yore, and this doubt was strengthened

[1] Dr. Gustav Adolf Keferstein (1799-1861), pastor, and a standard writer on music. He wrote under the names K. Stein (Schumann chose this name for the dedication of some songs), and Dr. Peregrinus Jocosus.

by a recent remark of yours in the Stuttgart paper. You said there that it was only by the study of Bach and Kuhnau[1] that one could understand how Mozart and Haydn came by their music, and that it remains a mystery how the more modern composers came by theirs, or words to that effect. I cannot entirely agree with you. Mozart and Haydn only knew Bach through extracts. The effect he might have had on their productive power, had they known him in all his greatness, is inconceivable. On the other hand, modern music, with its intricacies, its poetry and humour, has its origin chiefly in Bach. Mendelssohn, Bennett, Chopin, Hiller, all the so-called Romanticists (speaking of Germans only), stand much nearer to Bach than to Mozart in their music. They know Bach thoroughly, one and all. I myself make my daily confession to this high-priest with a view to purifying and strengthening my musical nature. Then, again, Kuhnau must not be placed on a line with Bach, however estimable and delightful he may be. Had Bach written nothing but the *Wohltemperirtes Klavier*, he would still be worth a hundred of Kuhnau. In fact, I consider Bach to be quite unapproachable, immeasurable by ordinary standards.[2]

[1] Johann Kuhnau (1660-1722), Bach's predecessor as choirmaster at the Thomas Kirche, Leipzig. He composed learned works for the pianoforte.

[2] In the *Neue Folge* (p. 178) of Schumann's letters the passage reads: 'Had Kuhnau written nothing,' etc., an obvious misprint, unless there is a slip of the pen in Schumann's original.

And now I have a great favour to ask, and can think of no one better able or more likely to help me than yourself. But promise me, my dear Keferstein, to let no third person into the secret.

You will perhaps know of my engagement to Clara; also, possibly, the —— means her father has employed to prevent our union. . . . Well, he may be able to delay it for a time, but it is not in his power to prevent it ultimately. Clara's very considerable position in the musical world has often given me cause to reflect on my own less established footing. Convinced as I am of her disinterestedness in loving me for my music and myself alone, I still think it would please her if I attained a higher social rank. This brings me to my inquiry. Can you tell me if it is difficult to take a doctor's degree at Jena; what examination I should have to pass, if any; and to whom I can apply for information? Would not my post as editor of an important paper of seven years' standing, my position as a composer and the activity I have displayed in various undertakings, be of some account in the matter? Tell me your real opinion, and please remember my request for strict silence on the matter at present. . . .

59.

To Keferstein.

LEIPZIG, *February* 8, 1840.

. . . I should like to secure my doctor's degree on one of two conditions. I could qualify for it by writing a treatise, which would be an arduous task, or the diploma might be made out to me in recognition of my past services as composer and author, which would be by far the more pleasing and satisfactory way. Help me once more with your sage advice. I know very little Latin, but I think I should be equal to a solid German treatise. I am at present engaged in collecting material for an essay on Shakespeare in his relation to music. It is to deal with his allusions to it, his qualifying remarks, and his manner of introducing the subject in his dramas—a wide and fascinating study. This would, of course, take some time, as it would mean reading through the whole of his works. If you consider an essay unnecessary, or think this particular one unsuitable, you will perhaps be willing, out of sympathy for Clara and myself, to try and obtain the diploma for me on the grounds of my earlier writings. To this intent I make bold to send you a batch of articles, written either by myself or by others with reference to me, which I have selected at random in a great hurry. I also enclose some diplomas, and will send, if desired, a testimonial from the authorities here as to my character and the *curriculum vitæ*, not forgetting the customary fees of which you reminded me. As a crowning favour you might, perhaps, go and see the deacon[1] and put in a good word for me. You could then explain to him my position in the musical world, the relation in which I stand to

[1] Reinhold.

Clara—since it is no longer a secret—the suffering which her father has caused us, and the particular significance and value of the title to me at this moment, when people are saying the wildest things about us. In a word, I want not only to be able to say I have taken this and that degree, but to have my special claim to the honour stated in the diploma. I am told that a respected Leipzig theologian obtained a degree from your University in some such way—that is, without any dissertation, but by payment of the usual fees. Is this true?

One more question. Will the degree be a musical one in either case? I should prefer that, of course. I shall be glad if you can tell me what *form* the diploma will take. Let me thank you on Clara's behalf and my own. We may soon, I hope, be able to bring our thanks in person if you do not come and pay us a visit first.

I shall be sending on your last letter, one of these days, to Clara, who is at present with her mother at Hamburg. She will probably write herself to thank you for your kind words to me about her. She is, indeed, all that you paint her—a rare creature, comprising in herself innumerable fine qualities.

The enclosed portrait is intended to freshen up your recollection of me. Please look on it kindly. It is not quite perfect as a likeness, though drawn by a great artist,[1] a proof that even a master-hand

[1] Kriehuber.

is not infallible. Still, I think the general effect is good. Please do not hang me among a crowd of critical Leipzig and Stuttgart 'doctors,' but put me next to Sebastian Bach (what would I not give to hear him play the organ!), then I shall begin to improvise. . . .

60.

To Keferstein.

LEIPZIG, *February* 19, 1840.

. . . Do you know that I have written four hundred pages of music during the last two years? Most of it is published, too. When I consider that my music has nothing mechanical about it, but makes inconceivable demands on my heart, it seems only natural that the heart should need rest after such exertions.

My editorial duties can only fill a secondary place, great as is my devotion to the paper. Is it not our most sacred duty to cultivate our talents? I remember your writing to me some years ago to this effect, and have plodded on bravely ever since. This by way of justification, my dear friend, for your last lines contained a certain reflection, as I gathered, on the way in which I fulfil my editorial duties. I really do not deserve this, for the very reason that I am so much occupied with other work, and because this other work is of greater importance, being, in fact, my life-work. Here I am at this moment, fresh from composing. I am doing nothing but vocal music of all sorts just now, including some quartets for male voices, which I should like to dedicate to the friend who reads these lines, if he will kindly promise to make no further attempt to distract me from composing. May I? I can hardly describe to you the pleasure of vocal—as compared with instrumental—writing, and the tempest of ideas that surges within me as I sit at work. I have had some entirely new ideas, and am even meditating an opera, though that is impossible so long as I edit the paper. . . .

61.

To Keferstein.

LEIPZIG, *February* 29, 1840.

My satisfaction is now complete. The eulogy[1] is so impressive that I suspect I have you to thank for it. It has given the greatest satisfaction to me and to my friends. A copy was sent first thing, of course, to a certain young lady who is still enough of a child to jump for joy at her new dignity in being betrothed to Dr. Schumann. She is sure to write and thank you herself, but you will have to wait until she goes to Berlin for the signed portrait. She keeps all her things there. The journey to Copenhagen, on which I was to have accompanied her and her mother, will probably be given up, as she dreads the crossing so very much. There is still a possibility of it, how-

[1] In the doctor's diploma.

ever. In any case, I shall soon see her, and I need hardly tell you what glorious times we shall have together at the piano and elsewhere. . . .

62.

To Keferstein.

LEIPZIG, *August* 24, 1840.

MY VERY DEAR FRIEND,

Many thanks for your gratifying account,[1] by which you enabled me to enjoy it all at a distance. I always hoped I might be coming to Jena one of these days, but it is not to be. Clara has gone from Weimar to Bad Liebenstein, near Eisenach, to stay with her friend, Emilia List, who wrote to her unexpectedly from there. She is to stay there for the few weeks left before our wedding, and will not break her journey on the way back, so I have given up my plan of going to meet her at Weimar by way of Jena. There are now—God helping us—no further obstacles in the way of our wedding, as you feared. I had the bliss of hearing the second reading of our banns yesterday. Clara is also blissfully happy, as you may imagine. The trials we underwent were really too humiliating. Clara wrote enthusiastically of her stay with you at Jena, and I was hardly less delighted at hearing of the way in which you fêted her. Your article brings me a fresh proof of your kindly feeling, though parts of it, especially

[1] Of a concert given by Clara at Jena, on August 8.

those concerning me, seem to me—if you will not misunderstand the phrase—too enthusiastic. If it were signed by its kind author I should have no doubts about accepting it, but this, of course, I do not for a moment expect of you in your position. The public is always inclined to see a friend's services in any unsigned enthusiastic notice, and when their suspicions are correct (as in this case, for are you not our dear good friend?) they like to have the friend's name as a guarantee of good faith. But, however that may be, your sympathy does my heart good. I hope my subsequent works will at least not tend to diminish it. If you really wish to honour Clara and myself with public recognition, the *Frankfurter Journal* would be a good medium, though I fear the editors take but little interest in us foreigners. Try them, anyway, my dear friend; if they refuse, I should suggest an evening or society paper.

I am, I confess, too proud to make use of the Härtels to influence Fink. All ingenious attempts on the artist's part to stimulate public opinion are detestable to me. Good stuff will always make its way. Not that I am indifferent to thorough and intelligent criticism, believe me; but the artist is not the one to instigate it. Clara is like me in this, much as she delights in, and *actually needs*, encouragement. She is indeed subject to fits of depression, which are quite inexplicable to me. I have had to rally her about it more than once.

But enough of that. It is perhaps hardly necessary to add the assurance that I am enjoying to the full my present happiness and my glorious expectations. I have had to make Clara a formal promise to accompany her to St. Petersburg, as she threatened to go alone if I refused. I believe she would really have done so, for she is quite indifferent to appearances. You will spare me the portrayal of my unwillingness to leave my quiet circle. I will only say that it distresses me greatly to think of it. Yet I must not let Clara see it. The change will be good for her from the physical point of view, for, slender as she is, she is very healthy, and has the endurance of a man.

BOOK II

THE FIGHT FOR CLARA (1836-1840)

'I will say no more of my happiness in possessing a girl with whom I have grown to be one through art, intellectual affinities, the regular intercourse of years, and the deepest and holiest affection. My whole life is one joyous activity.'—*To* EDUARD *and* KARL SCHUMANN, *March* 19, 1838.

'No maiden, no angel from heaven, could be truer to me than you are; you alone could love me thus with a love so inexpressibly noble. I have no words for you; only a peep into my dreams could show you my thoughts of you. I hardly know what to say, but I have the beautiful consciousness of having been myself scrupulously true to you.'—*To* CLARA, *February* 23, 1839.

INTRODUCTION

SINCE music has so often been praised as the herald of love, as its special art and language, is there any wonder that in the history of music, and still more in the biographies of musicians, the passion is displayed under so many aspects? Of all the stories and legends of love or marriage between musicians, whatever their human or their artistic interest, from J. S. Bach and his enthusiastic singer, Anna Magdalena, to Richard Wagner and Liszt's brilliant daughter Cosima—none offers so perfect a model as the union of Clara Wieck and Robert Schumann.

I do not believe that a similarly perfect example is to be found in the whole annals of art. Not only was each the heart's choice of the other, not only was it on either side the bitter-sweet love of youth, which touches the extremes of joy and despair—but they fought a hard fight in evil days before their happiness was won. They were two noble souls, distinguished by fastidious purity and true excellence of character—two buoyant minds consecrated to the service of art. And, to fill the measure of their happiness, they served the same art. Their marriage fairly symbolizes the union of the male and female elements in creative art. It is wonderful to observe how they adapted themselves one to the other; how the man's artistic production was inspired and intensified by the woman's presence, and how her reproductive art reached its supreme excellence through his works. She was the ideal interpreter of her husband's music, and to her he entrusted his finest conceptions. May it not almost be called an actual marriage between the arts?

From Schumann's letters and those of his friends we gain a fair conception of their wedded happiness, but we find the real basis for our conclusions in the standard biography of *Clara Schumann* (Breitkopf and Härtel, Leipzig, 1903-1905), by Berthold Litzmann, who is to be envied for his pleasant task. He may well say on his title-page, 'from diaries and letters,' for further reference was practically unnecessary. The diaries offer peculiarly interesting material in as great abundance as could be desired. There are in all forty-seven quarto volumes, which form an almost unbroken narrative of Clara Schumann's life, from her birth to the beginning of her last illness. True, her father made the greater proportion of the entries up to her nineteenth birthday (1838), but sufficient letters are available to give a vivid individual picture of her. Her father's collaboration throws some light on his own character, which, though insufficient to explain his strange subsequent behaviour, prevents us from conceiving him to be merely a madman or a criminal. Although made up of genuine letters and diaries which chronicle experiences and emotions, this book has all the fascination of an exciting novel, in which the art of the story-teller makes the joys and sorrows of his characters seem part of our personal experience. The personages of the drama might have stepped out of a novel. Between the hero and the heroine stands the lady's father, hard as stone, inexorable. The unfortunate girl has to choose between her father, to whom she owes everything and for whom she has a deep filial affection, and her lover, whom her father first rejects for no apparent reason, then repels with violence, and finally treats as a deadly enemy. Always capricious, but otherwise a man of strong and upright character, her father descends to heartless tyranny, and even to slander, as he sees his daughter, after her first hesitation and doubt, become more and more confirmed in her devotion to her lover. The whole affair is a puzzle. Schumann had proved the steadfastness of his love; his powers were gaining increasing recognition, and he was able to offer his wife an assured future. Why, then, did this estimable teacher persist in opposing his daughter's marriage with the composer? The conclusion drawn from many passages in the letters is that the old man was actuated by sheer jealousy and avarice. Yet, if he had consistently encouraged rich or aristocratic suitors, he had also favoured the pretensions of an ordinary piano teacher. This embittered struggle, which eventually became a tragi-comedy to the onlookers, was a real tragedy to the father—a tragedy to the artist in him.

Friedrich Wieck (1785-1873) remains one of the greatest pianoforte teachers of all time. He was not only absolutely conscientious, but passionately attached to his calling. In presenting his daughter to the world as a finished artist, he was peculiarly conscious of achieving his masterpiece. Even before her birth he had determined that, if a girl, she should become a great pianist, and should receive the name Clara as a presage of her brilliant destiny. He witnessed the splendid accomplishment of his task. The whole world paid tribute to his child; he saw in her neither a phenomenal talent, nor a prodigy of iron diligence, but his own handiwork. She was both daughter and pupil. Then he saw her growing love for Robert Schumann, who had also been his pupil, but had only used Wieck's school as a means to higher ends. Schumann's nature was inaccessible to pedagogic instruction. His creative genius and native superiority of talent was to Wieck, whose art was purely reproductive, a standing reminder of his own creative impotence. Wieck knew well enough that once Clara became Schumann's wife, she would no longer take her art from her father direct. Had Schumann's music resembled that of Kalkbrenner, Herz, Hünten, or others of their fellows—music which is only effective in the hands of virtuosi—the case would have been different. He, however, wrote music which offered little scope for technical display but entirely captivated genuine artists. Wieck knew his daughter far too well not to foresee her whole-hearted enthusiasm for Schumann's music. He fought for the artist, not for the daughter. The artist was in a far higher degree his work; his creative power found its fullest expression in her. Could he see his work, the product of his own art, lost under the influence of another's personality and cease to exist, except in interpreting the creations of another man?

Such was the nature of this often misunderstood and misrepresented struggle. The artist Wieck fought to retain possession of his own masterpiece. We must forgive the artist the faults of the man and the father.

The quarrel was fought out between these three principals. The others who were involved in it played no essential part, interesting as their rôles sometimes were. There was the gallery of the suitors whom the father inflicted on his daughter; also a Dr. Schilling, a wolf in sheep's clothing, who insinuated himself into the unsuspecting maiden's confidence by a pretended sympathy. But there were true friends who helped the lovers. The most touching figure is that of the elderly maid, Johanna Strobel, who was so taciturn that it was long before the girl ventured to confide in her, in spite of her constant and unmistakable love and fidelity to the motherless child.

But the best part of the picture is formed by the lovers themselves, particularly by the woman, for in this union the woman had the stronger, one might almost say the more masculine soul. Clara was nine, when Schumann, at the age of eighteen (1828), became her father's pupil. The two soon became firm friends. He used to tell her fairy-tales; even as a child she fascinated the artist in him, and her playing soon inspired him to compose. She quickly gained the fame which greets the virtuoso from all sides, while he painfully struggled up the thorny path of creative art. He formed an earlier attachment which proved mistaken, before he recognized that he felt more than friendship for the child in Wieck's house; while her girlish precocity enabled her to realize what she seemed to be losing.

In November, 1835, they discovered their love for one another. Eventually they were able to marry on September 12, 1840, without the blessing of Clara's surly father, but with the full consent of her mother, who was separated from Wieck, and to whom the girl turned in her desolation.

The lovers' correspondence during these five years is one of the prose poems of German literature. It contains all the sweetness of young love, the stolen meetings and greetings, kisses snatched on the threshold. Then came the bitter separation; the father's veto soon fell. They were never to see one another again. Secret letters followed. Robert Schumann wrote on one occasion (Letter 84): 'It gives me moral strength to see my dear girl so brave.' We may apply his words more generally. It really is inspiring to watch her fighting for her love, without sentimentalism or femininity, but with the finest and purest womanly heroism. Her loyalty never wavered for a moment, but this was the least of her virtues. She endured uncomplainingly the tortures which her father inflicted with—there is no other word for it—execrable malice. She consoled her lover, who was often driven from his bliss to the blackest depths of despair and bitterness by their wretched position. But through her sorrows she ripened to magnificent womanhood, and became the incomparable artist whose peculiar charm has been best celebrated by Franz Grillparzer, after she had, at the age of nineteen, interpreted to the world the beauties of Beethoven's F minor sonata.

> 'A wizard, weary of the world and life,
> Locked up the treasures of his magic art
> Within a casket, strong and firmly sealed,
> Then threw the key upon the waves, and died.
> The smaller men bestirred themselves in vain,
> No tool was strong enough to force the seal,
> And master and enchantment slept alike.
> A shepherd maiden, playing by the sea,
> Looked on at the profane and eager search,
> With wise, unconscious eyes, as children do;
> Dipped her white fingers in the flowing tide,
> Grasped something, raised it, and the key was found!
> Then she sprang up, with wildly beating heart;
> The casket glowed before her as with life.
> The key is in, and turned; the lid flies open;
> The imprisoned spirits, rising, owned her charm
> And innocence; then moved obedient
> To the touch of her white fingers as she played.'

Her love grew deeper as her artistic powers ripened. 'I feel more and more,' she wrote, 'that my life is for you only; all else is indifferent to me except my art, which springs from you.' Indeed, although she at first seemed almost his superior, she rapidly recognized and did homage to his creative genius. 'I am astonished at your mind, at all the new treasures it contains—do you know, I am sometimes afraid of you, and wonder if it is really true that such a genius is to be my husband? I am at times overtaken by the idea that I can never prove sufficient for you, though it is possible you may love me none the less for that.' She was, at the time of writing, an artist of world-wide fame, he an unknown musician. But she not only comprehended his genius; she was, in the best sense of the word, his muse. He often expressed himself in a similar way, as in the letter accompanying the *Novelletten* (1839): 'Dearest, in the *Novelletten* are my thoughts of you in every possible position and circumstance and all your irresistibleness! Yes, I mean it! No one could have written the *Novelletten* unless he had gazed into such eyes and touched such lips as yours—in short, another may very well do better work, but nothing just like these.'

We ourselves breathe more freely when the two are at last united. We know that Clara's married life has trouble in store, trouble of the worst kind—the loss of the loved husband in the most cruel circumstances, since intellectual death was to seize him before the dissolution of the bodily life. She bore this fate also in the spirit of the words she had written in her diary on her wedding day—words that form a fitting close to her girlhood: 'A period of my life ends here: if I have experienced trouble in my early years, there has been much happiness which I shall never forget. Now another life is beginning, life in him whom I love beyond all else and beyond my own self. But my responsibilities are heavy, too; may Heaven give me strength to fulfil them as a good wife should. God has always been, and will continue to be, my helper. I have always had perfect trust in Him, which I shall ever preserve.'

For the purpose of the present book this most emotional period of Schumann's life is seen from his side only, mirrored in his soul. The line 'Himmelhoch jauchzend, zum Tode betrübt' is doubly comprehensible in the case of this susceptible nature. Even Clara, who was far more courageous in her attitude towards life, testifies in her letters to the terrible emotional storms through which the two had to pass. Attempts have often been made to present Wieck's behaviour in a better light.[1]

In particular, Wieck's surviving daughter, Marie, has aroused controversy with regard to Litzmann's book—quite unjustly, as, after a thorough examination of all the circumstances, the eminent writer Gustav Jansen has shown in the preface to the second edition of the *Briefe Robert Schumanns* (Leipzig, 1904). All this only serves to throw into relief the bright figures of the lovers.

In these letters the principle of selection must be even more rigidly enforced than in the earlier extracts, if the main lines of Schumann's development are to remain clear, for many of the letters run to the length of a little book.

63.

Robert to Clara.

En route for Zwickau *after* 10 *p.m.,*
February 13, 1836.

I can hardly keep my eyes open. For the last two hours I have been waiting for the express mail-coach. The roads are so bad that it may be two o'clock before we get away. How vividly I can see you, my own beloved Clara. You seem so

[1] Kohut, *Fr. Wieck: Ein Lebens- und Künstlerbild,* 1888; Joss, *Fr. Wieck und sein Verhältnis zu Schumann,* 1900.

near that I imagine I could almost touch you. There was a time when I could express my attachment in pretty phrases; but I can do so no longer. So, if you did not know it, I should never be able to tell you. You must love me a great deal, too, you know. I ask much, because I give much.

To-day has been a day of varied emotions, bringing me, as it did, my mother's will, and accounts of her death.[1] But through the darkness I discern your fair image, and my burden is lightened.

I may as well tell you that my future is now on a much more certain footing. I must not, of course, sit down with folded hands, and have still much to accomplish if I would win the image you see in your mirror. You too, unlike Gräfin Rossi,[2] will want to carry on your art, to share my work and my burdens, my joy and my sorrow. Write me your ideas on the matter.

My first effort in Leipzig will be to bring order into my material affairs; with myself I am at peace. Perhaps your father will, after all, not refuse his blessing when I ask it. There is a great deal to think over still, but meanwhile I trust in our good angel. Fate designed us for one another, as I have known for a long time, though I was not bold enough to speak to you sooner or to come to an understanding.

I will give you a fuller explanation later on of

[1] Died February 4, 1836.

[2] Henriette Sontag had married Graf Rossi in 1828.

my rough jottings to-day, and if you cannot read it—why, then, at least be sure I love you more than I can say. It is getting very dark in this room, and my fellow-passengers are sleeping. Outside there is a snowstorm. For my part I shall take refuge in a corner, bury my head in a cushion, and think of nothing but you. Farewell, my own Clara.

Your

ROBERT.

64.

To Clara Wieck.

August 13, 1837.

Are you loyal and true as ever? My confidence in you is indeed unassailable, but the stoutest heart would be disconcerted when left without a word from the dearest thing in the world, which is what you are to me. I have turned the matter over in my mind a thousand times, and everything tells me that it must come to pass if we make up our minds to carry it through. Let me have just one word, 'yes,' from you if you are willing to hand your father a letter[1] from me on your birthday (September 13). He is kindly disposed to me just now, and will not repulse me if you plead for me too.

I write this just as the dawn is breaking. Would that there were only one more sunrise to part us! Remember, above all, that it must come to pass if we make up our minds to carry it through.

[1] See Letter 65.

Say nothing of this letter to anyone; it might spoil everything. And do not forget that 'yes.' I must have this assurance before I can think of anything further. All this comes straight from my heart, word for word, and here is my signature to it—

ROBERT SCHUMANN.

Clara to Robert.

LEIPZIG, *August* 15, 1837.

So one little 'yes' is all you want? What an important little word it is! Surely a heart so full of inexpressible love as mine can utter it freely. I can indeed say it. My inmost soul whispers it unceasingly to you.

Could I put into words my heart's anguish, my many tears? No, it is beyond my power. But the fates may permit us to meet before long, and then——! Your proposal seems daring to me, but love takes small heed of danger, and again I say 'yes.' Surely God will not turn my eighteenth birthday into a day of trouble? He could not be so cruel. For a long time I have shared your conviction: 'it must come to pass.' Nothing shall make me waver. I will prove to my father that a youthful [heart] can be firm.

In great haste,

Your

CLARA.

65.

To F. Wieck (*delivered* September 13, 1837).

What I have to say to you is so simple, and yet the right words may sometimes fail me. It is difficult to control a pen with so trembling a hand. I must therefore ask your indulgence for any possible negligence in style or expression.

To-day is Clara's birthday, the day on which the dearest object my world holds saw the light, the day on which I have always indulged in retrospect since I felt myself so closely bound up with her. I confess that to-day I am able to face the future more calmly than ever before. I am assured—in all human probability—against want, full of pleasant projects, able to champion any noble cause with youthful enthusiasm, capable of work and conscious of glorious opportunities, strong in the hope of using my talents to the full, and rich in esteem and affection—surely these things might suffice! But alas! it is not so. What do all these weigh against the pain of being separated from the one who provides the motive for all my activities, the one who so loyally reciprocates my love! You, her happy father, know this incomparable girl well enough. Read in her face the truth of my words.

Your testing of me during the past eighteen months has been severe as the hand of fate itself. But how can I bear you ill-will! I offended you deeply, but my penance has been heavy too. Put me on my trial for as long again ; I may perhaps be able to meet your wishes and regain your confidence, if you do not ask impossibilities. You know my power of endurance where great ends are in question. If, then, you are satisfied that I am a man to be trusted in every respect, will you not set the seal of your fatherly sanction upon our covenant, and thereby complete our happiness? My feeling towards Clara, which thrills in every fibre of my being, is no passing desire, no violent emotion, no surface thing, but the deep-rooted conviction that everything augurs well for the happiness of our union—a conviction founded on Clara's power to secure happiness for us both. Does not her noble nature diffuse it everywhere? If you admit this, you will surely promise me to arrange nothing definite as to Clara's future. I, for my part, give you my word not to communicate with her without your permission. I only ask that we may be allowed to write when you are away on long tours.

Now that this vital question has found utterance I can again breathe freely, knowing myself to be full of good-will towards all men. I lay my future confidently in your hands. You owe it to my position, my talent and my character to give me a considerate and decisive answer. It would be most satisfactory if we could talk it over.

The moments which pass between now and then will be charged with the same emotion as that which thrills us when we listen for the thunderclap after the flash, and tremble to know if it portends annihilation or a blessing. May your decision bring a blessing! I implore you, with a heart beating with love and fear, to renew your friendship with one of your oldest friends, and prove yourself the best possible father to the best of children.

ROBERT SCHUMANN.

Enclosure to Frau Wieck.

Let me, above all, enlist your sympathy, my dear lady, on behalf of our future. I know that there is nothing of the step-mother in your attitude. Your clear-sightedness and kindly disposition, your genuine respect and love for Clara, will help you to find a way. We should all think it a calamity if the birthday of one who has contributed to the happiness of so many people should be turned into a day of sorrow. Will you not try to avert it?

Yours sincerely,

R. SCHUMANN.

Enclosure to Clara.

After our most painful separation, dear Clara, you will, I know, support me lovingly in all that I have said to your parents, and raise your voice where my words seem inadequate.[1]

Your

R. S.

[1] Wieck neither gave Clara these lines, nor showed her the other two letters.

66.

To Ernst A. Becker.

LEIPZIG, *September* 14, 1837.

DEAR FRIEND,

W[ieck]'s answer was so confused, so perplexing a mixture of refusal and consent that I am at a loss—absolutely—to know what to do. If only you could have been here for a few minutes, or were here now, so that he could talk to some one who might succeed in overcoming his vanity (for such it seemed to me) on certain points. He seems bent on Clara's being a concert pianist all her life. Naturally, he can produce no valid objection, and it was, as I say, impossible to find out his real meaning. I have had no chance of speaking to Clara; my only hope is in her firmness. Will you not write a few lines to Wieck, making clear to him his great responsibility? I should like to see the letter first—but do as you think best. Tell him I showed you my letter to him, etc. I am deeply depressed and incapable of thought.

67.

Robert to Clara.

September 18, 1837.

My interview with your father was terrible. He was frigid, hostile, confused and contradictory at once. Truly his method of stabbing is original, for he drives in the hilt as well as the blade. . . .

Well, and what now, my dear Clara? I am

at a loss—absolutely—to know what to do. My reasoning power is quite exhausted, and any display of feeling is worse than useless in dealing with your father. What in the world can we do? You must be particularly on your guard against any attempt he may make *to sell you*. . . . I believe in you—God knows—with all my heart. This is, indeed, my chief support. But you will have more need of strength than you suspect. Did not your father give me the grim assurance to my face that he was 'not to be shaken'? You must be prepared for anything, for if he cannot succeed by force he will employ cunning. Be prepared for anything, I repeat.

I feel so lifeless, so *humiliated*, to-day that I am incapable of a single fine thought. Even your picture is so blurred that I almost forget what your eyes are like. I am not so reduced in spirit as to think of giving you up, but so embittered by this outrage to my most sacred feelings, by being treated like one of the common herd. If I could only have a word from you! Tell me what I must do. If I do not hear from you, the mockery of the whole thing will drive me to flight. To think that I am not allowed to see you! He will only allow it in some public place, where we should be a laughing-stock for everybody. What a cold sting there is in all this! He further permits us to correspond when you are travelling, and that is the sum total of his concessions. . . . I always considered your father a good and humane person, but

I look in vain for anything that might excuse him, in vain for any nobler reason underlying his refusal, such as a fear that your artistic career might suffer through an early engagement, the plea that you are too young, or any similar objection. No sign of anything of the sort! Believe me, he will fling you at the first suitor who comes, provided he has money and titles enough. It is as if he could conceive of nothing higher than touring and concert-giving. To this end he would sacrifice your heart's blood and cripple my strength at the moment when I am striving to do great things in the world, over and above which he mocks at all your tears.

Your ring is looking at me in such a charming way, as if it would chide me for reproaching my Clara's father. The word 'steadfast,' which you uttered three times the other day, seemed to come from the very depths of your soul. That day did so much for me, Clara; don't be angry if I am weak to-day and have hurt your father's feelings. I have right on my side.

Remember what is at stake. Exert yourself to the utmost, and if your gentleness fails, use your strength. Silence seems to be my only refuge, for every new attempt to persuade your father would provoke fresh insult. Do all you can to find a way out; I will follow like a child. . . . How my poor head swims! I could laugh for very anguish. This cannot go on much longer—my health will not stand it. . . . God preserve me from despair. My life is torn up by the roots.

(In the afternoon of the same day.)

I think we have lost no ground, though we have gained little enough. I am vexed now that I wrote, and wish I had waited eight or ten weeks. I can see the importance of advancing slowly and cautiously. He must, after all, one day give in to the idea of losing you. His obstinacy must give way before our love, my own Clara. We *must* win! . . .

You must disabuse your father of his various mistaken ideas. . . . He admitted that we should be the most blissful pair in the world when I put it to him, but farther than that he would not go. He went on to say that we should want much more money than we thought, and named an enormous sum, whereas we have precisely as much as a hundred of the most respected families here. Don't let him argue you out of that. Then he said you would often weep in secret if we did not give big receptions, and so on. Clara, is that true, or only a jest?

He had no valid objection to bring forward, and can have none, for right and reason are on our side. If he drives us to extremities by persisting in refusing his consent for a year and a half or two years more, we must take the law into our own hands. . . . In that case a magistrate would marry us. Heaven send it may not come to that! . . . Let me have a few soothing, kind words soon. My picture of you is much clearer and lovelier now than when I wrote this morning, and your thrice repeated 'steadfast' is a message from heaven's blue. Before I take leave of you to-day, my beloved, swear to me once more by your eternal happiness that you have courage to bear the trials laid upon us, even as I make the same vow at this moment, raising two fingers of my right hand. I will not give you up—trust me! God help us!

Ever your own

ROBERT.

Send this back without delay, on your honour.

Clara to Robert.

LEIPZIG, 1837.

(In Robert's writing: 'Read September 26, with indescribable delight.)

Do you still doubt me? I must forgive you, for, of course, I am only a weak girl. Weak, yes; but my soul is strong, and my heart steadfast and unchanging. Let this be enough to destroy all your doubts.

I have been very unhappy up to now, but send me a few words of comfort under these lines, and I shall face the world serenely. I have promised Father to be happy, and to devote myself to my art and the public for some years more. You will hear all sorts of reports of me, and many a doubt will arise in your mind; but when you hear this, that, or the other, say to yourself, 'She does it all for me.' If you should ever waver, you would break the heart of one who loves once for all.

CLARA.

(*Outside*) Send me back these lines. Do it for my peace of mind.

68.

Robert to Clara.

LEIPZIG, 1837.

Such heavenly words I cannot return. Besides, they are safe enough in my keeping. Not another word of the past, but let us keep our eyes fixed on our life's single aim. Trust me, my beloved Clara, and let the conviction of my strength strengthen you in all your trials. One last request before I let you go: Will you not venture on 'thee' and 'thou' when you write to me? You must often have used them in thought.[1] Are you not my passionately loved, affianced one, some day to be—— Well, just one kiss, and good-bye.

Your

ROBERT.

69.

Robert to Clara.

LEIPZIG, *October* 3, 1837.

. . . It might happen that we heard nothing of one another for a time, that your father inter-

[1] Schumann had used the intimate form of address for the first time in the end of the preceding letter. From this time onwards the lovers wrote 'thee' and 'thou.' [Tr.]

cepted our letters, or even that they blackened my character to you. If they should say I had forgotten you or what not, never believe a word of it. It is a wicked world, but we must try to keep ourselves unsmirched. If I could count on a letter from you every two months, it would be a great comfort. Is that asking too much? In three hours I shall see you, and I am in terror. It is the last time—perhaps for ever. . . .

70.

Robert to Clara.

LEIPZIG, *November* 8, 1837, *early morning.*

So you only want one line! You shall have more, although I should like to be angry with you, as, indeed, you deserve. I never thought you could keep silence so long. I could not have done it in your place, for you can always convey letters to me, though I cannot to you. What I have suffered these last few days I will not say. Then, yesterday your letter came. It was as if I had escaped a great disaster. Short as it is, it comes from you, and is a message from your heart. Thank you, dear! Your father has written to me to this effect: 'You are an excellent person, but not so excellent as some. I don't quite know what I mean to do with Clara, but—hearts! What do I care about hearts?' etc.

I will copy out two passages for you: 'Rather than see two such artists settle down to housekeeping and petty anxieties, I would sacrifice my daughter alone in one way or another.' Then comes this magnificent sentence: 'If I have to marry my daughter without delay to some one else, you will only have yourself to thank.' This last, my dear Clara, is sufficiently final and decisive. What can I do with such a letter? I must either leave it unanswered, or tell him the truth; there can be no further relation between us. What have I to do with a man like that? I admit it is serious, and I cannot think how it will all end. Can you really hold out? Shall you ever have a return of last Tuesday's mood? You won't be angry, my dearest girl, but I can't help telling you that you said some things that evening which you ought not to have said, because it made you unhappy and me too. Are you not content to be mine? Are you not convinced that you are going to be the happiest of wives? If not, you had better break our bond now. I will give you back everything—the ring too. But if you are happy in my love, if it fills your whole heart, and if you have weighed my faults and bad ways, and are content with the little I can offer you besides (which does not include pearls and diamonds), then we keep to the old love, my faithful Clara, then I shall never give you back anything, nor ever release you from your promise to me, insisting to the full on all the claims which your consent and your ring give me.

Store this up in your heart. Doubt is in itself

faithlessness; trust, the half of possession. We may leave the rest to our guardian angel, who destined us each for the other in our cradles.

I ask you, further, to save all my letters, and to promise me on your honour never to show them (as in a weak moment at Dresden) to your father; to remember always your duty to yourself as well as to your father, who has had so much pleasure through you, and has in return made the last years of your life wretched; and, finally, never to forget me.[1]

Think of me always at nine o'clock in the evening, the hour when I am always with you.

Farewell, my darling girl.

Your

ROBERT.

71.

Robert to Clara.

[*November*] 29.

To think that the paltry 200 silver pieces of which our yearly income falls short should cause all this fuss! They must be found, of course. You know what I have; the half of it I need myself, and if the other half is not enough for you, you could always earn something extra. Of course, it all depends upon how we set up housekeeping, and I will tell you at once my ideas about it. I should like best to keep my present independent position for a time, with a pretty house not far out of town. Then, with you beside me, I

[1] This paragraph is italicized in the original.

should work in bliss and peace. You would still practise your noble art, but less for the public and for the sake of gain than for the favoured few and for our own happiness—that is, if you are content. A life such as this would not mean any great outlay. Whether it would entirely satisfy you, and continue to do so, I know no more than you do yourself. We all change, and our plans are often wrecked by chance, fate, or outward interference. But this is, as I say, the life I would choose. I might paint everything in still more alluring colours, so that you would fall on my neck and say, 'Yes, this is the life for us, Robert.' Do this for yourself, if you love me.

It would be quite another thing if you were anxious to keep yourself before the public. I should still be content, but I should propose shutting up our house for three months in the year (I could get away for that length of time, even if I still edited the paper), and travelling [little or not at all in Germany], to Paris or London. Your name is known everywhere, while I have a crowd of friends and connexions, so you see we could not fail to reap laurels and earn money, and should return, laden with the spoil, to that house which is still in the clouds. Leipzig would be the best centre for the execution of either of these plans—for the brilliant sunlight of publicity or the gentle moonlight of home life. . . . Even supposing this life failed to satisfy us, what should you say if, one morning, I announced to you, 'My dear wife, I have composed, unknown to you, excellent symphonies and other important works, and am ready to fly to the uttermost ends of the earth. You seem greedy of honour and glory, too, so how would it be if we packed up our diamonds, and settled in Paris?' You would say, 'Well, it's worth considering!' or, 'What an idea!' or, 'As you like'; or, perhaps, 'No, let us stay here; I am so happy,' on hearing which I should turn back to my writing-table, and go on writing.

May no one dispel these happy visions! Ah, when shall I have you for my very own! These nights of sleepless anguish, this tearless suffering endured for your sake—surely a kind Providence will one day give me compensation!

True, I have reckoned very much without my host—*i.e.*, your father—but there you must act. For the present I can do nothing. And this brings me to the point in my letter where I talked of insisting on my claims. You know, without being told, that I do not look upon our bond as a legal matter. Can you imagine I should hold you to it if you met another, luckier man, and loved him, with every prospect of being happy with him? Never! My love for you is too great, even should it mean my death-blow; my pride too strong, as you have had opportunity to judge. . . .

You say, rather unreasonably, that I jilted Ernestine. That is not true, for the bond was cancelled in due form by mutual consent. But some day I should like to tell you, in connexion with this dark page of my life, the secret of a serious physical complaint I once had; but this must wait for more leisure. It dates back to the summer of 1833, and you shall know it all some time. It is the key to all my actions and my peculiarities of character. Meanwhile, let me quote you a sentence I read lately at the end of a fine book: 'He is a fool who trusts his own heart—but judge not!'

. . . Once more, then, your consent, and your ring—the outward token of it—bind you undoubtedly . . . but no one can force you—I least of all—to be true to me. But you are a God-fearing, right-minded girl, and know all this perfectly. It was your own inexplicable remark that put me on to it.

. . . Oh, Clara, how sad it is that we are doomed to spend our best years apart. Wherever I go I hear nothing but praises of your beautiful self. I alone am debarred from talking to you, listening to you, while you have to exist on a few precious memories—such as our meeting on that first unforgettable evening in September—and little besides but trouble. You no longer delight in your ring, as you said on that hateful last page of your letter—the first of the kind, I admit! It is difficult to believe it comes from the same hand. You are passionate and reasonable, suspicious and trustful, loving and angry, by turns; in fact, you are the embodiment of Tuesday evening, with its moonlight, its tears of joy, and its surrender. Anyway, you have only to put on that cap of yours, and you can turn your weapon round and round in my heart, as you will—I shall not mind—while you wear the cap! Put it on sometimes, and tell yourself, 'That is how he loves me best.' My child, you understand me, don't you? It comes from my very heart, which is full of you. Your comment on your father's remark[1] is very consoling. I always write your name in the journal unwillingly, and should like to add: 'This is my dear love, about whom there is nothing to be said. She is no concern of yours at all. . . .' Don't you want to hear me play again? You know what characteristic queer middle parts I used to put, and how you used to stand beside me, watching my hand, while I looked into your eyes. We were spoiled in those days!

* * * * *

72.

Robert to Clara.

LEIPZIG, *December* 22, 1837.

Do you hear, among the thousand happy voices calling you, one who whispers your name? You look round and see me. 'You here, Robert?' you exclaim. And why not? I never leave you, but follow everywhere, though unseen. The figure fades away, but love and faith are unchanging.

[1] Wieck had complained that Schumann so seldom mentioned Clara in his paper.

New Year's Eve, 1837, *after* 11 *p.m.*

I have been sitting here a whole hour. Indeed, I meant to spend the whole evening writing to you, but no words would come. Sit down beside me now, slip your arm round me, and let us gaze peacefully, blissfully, into each other's eyes.

This world holds two lovers.

It is just striking the third quarter.

They are singing a chorale in the distance.

Tell me, do you know those two lovers? How happy we are, Clara! Let us kneel together, Clara, my Clara, so close that I can touch you, in this solemn hour.

On the morning of the 1*st*, 1838.

What a heavenly morning! All the bells are ringing; the sky is so golden and blue and clear—and before me lies your letter. I send you my first kiss, beloved.

The 2nd.

How happy your last letters have made me—those since Christmas Eve! I should like to call you by all the endearing epithets, and yet I can find no lovelier word than the simple word 'dear,' but there is a particular way of saying it. My dear one, then, I have wept for joy to think that you are mine, and often wonder if I deserve you. One would think that no one man's heart and brain could stand all the things that are crowded into one day. Where do these thousands of thoughts, wishes, sorrows, joys and hopes, come from? Day in, day out, the procession goes on. But how light-hearted I was yesterday and the day before! There shone out of your letters so noble a spirit, such faith, such a wealth of love! What would I not do for love of you, my own Clara! The knights of old were better off; they could go through fire or slay dragons to win their ladies, but we of to-day have to content ourselves with more prosaic methods, such as smoking fewer cigars, and the like. After all, though, we can love, knights or no knights; and so, as ever, only the times change, not men's hearts.

I have a hundred things to write to you, great and small, if only I could do it neatly, but my writing grows more and more indistinct, a sign, I fear, of heart weakness. There are terrible hours when your image forsakes me, when I wonder anxiously whether I have ordered my life as wisely as I might, whether I had any right to bind you to me, my angel, or can really make you as happy as I should wish. These doubts all arise, I am inclined to think, from your father's attitude towards me. It is so easy to accept other people's estimate of oneself. Your father's behaviour makes me ask myself if I am really so bad—of such humble standing—as to invite such treatment from anyone. Accustomed to easy victory over difficulties, to the smiles of fortune, and to affection, I have been spoiled by having things made too easy for me, and now I have to face refusal, insult, and calumny. I have read of many such things in novels, but I thought too highly of myself to imagine I could ever be the hero of a family tragedy of the Kotzebue sort myself. If I had ever done your father an injury, he might well hate me; but I cannot see why he should despise me and, as you say, hate me without any reason. But my turn will come, and I will then show him how I love you and himself; for I will tell you, as a secret, that I really love and respect your father for his many great and fine qualities, as no one but yourself can do. I have a natural inborn devotion and reverence for him, as for all strong characters, and it makes his antipathy for me doubly painful. Well, he may some time declare peace, and say to us, 'Take each other, then.'

You cannot think how your letter has raised and strengthened me. . . . You are splendid, and I have much more reason to be proud of you than you of me. I have made up my mind, though, to read all your wishes in your face. Then you will think, even though you don't say it, that your Robert is a really good sort, that he is entirely yours, and loves you more than words can say. You shall indeed have cause to think so in the happy future. I still see you as you looked in your little cap that last evening. I still hear you call me *du*. Clara, I heard nothing of what you said but that *du*. Don't you remember?

But I see you in many another unforgettable guise. Once you were in a black dress, going to the theatre with Emilia List; it was during our

Clara Schumann
1832

separation. I know you will not have forgotten ; it is vivid with me. Another time you were walking in the Thomasgässchen with an umbrella up, and you avoided me in desperation. And yet another time, as you were putting on your hat after a concert, our eyes happened to meet, and yours were full of the old unchanging love. I picture you in all sorts of ways, as I have seen you since. I did not look at you much, but you charmed me so immeasurably. . . . Ah, I can never praise you enough for yourself or for your love of me, which I don't really deserve.

Thursday, the 4th.

Your words, 'We shall soon be in Leipzig,' almost frighten me. I really dread seeing you both. Could you not arrange to stay in Dresden or somewhere ? Just think if we saw one another in the Rosental,[1] you sitting at a table and I fifty paces away ! That would be past bearing. . . . Really, unless we meet on a different footing, there will be no pleasure for me in your coming. Of course I want to see you again ! You will have grown a few more inches, I suppose. You are my own beautiful girl, and I cannot really blame your father for putting a high valuation on you. And once you begin to speak I quite lose my head. . . . Now, I have a confession to make. After your father's attitude to me, it seemed to me it would be —what shall I say ?—importunate, servile almost,

[1] A favourite walk outside Leipzig.

if I tried to win his favour (which is not my object) by the frequent mention of your name.[1] He would only rub his hands, and say, laughing, 'Is that how he hopes to win me over?' Dear, dear Clara, I know best, but you too know my great admiration for you, and the great respect with which I have always spoken of you; but I really cannot do this. Upon my word, I have no cause to do anything to please your father. Has he not ceased to show the smallest interest in me this long time past? Has he not hunted out and displayed all my failings to lower me in your estimation, and refused to recognize in me the qualities which he himself lacks? I will not cringe or give way to him one inch, neither will I beg for you at his hands. A certain letter of his to me contains expressions which I should hesitate about forgiving, should the Almighty Himself ask it of me. I was silent that once, remembering that he was your father; but the humiliation of it! I bore it once, but I could not do it again, even should it mean losing you. I assure you my disposition is towards gentleness and goodness, and my heart is still pure as it left the Creator's hands; but there is a limit to my patience, and I may yet show my claws. Forgive me all this. You will not be hurt. You are mine for always, and I yours. . . . And my plight is not desperate, since I can find protection under your outspread wings, my angel.

[1] In the *Zeitschrift*.

The 5th, evening.

. . . So the Kaiser has talked to you. Didn't he ask you: 'Do you know Signor Schumann?' And you answered: 'A little, your Majesty.' I wish I had been there. Will they make you an Imperial—Royal something or other?

Don't play quite so well, do you hear? Their enthusiasm must be kept within bounds, for with every storm of applause your father pushes me a little farther from you, remember. But, indeed, I am the last to grudge you your laurel wreaths, though they are but poor things compared to the myrtle garland I shall one day lay on your beautiful black hair. . . .

. . . The *Davidstänze* and the *Phantasiestücke* will be finished in a week. I will send you them, if you like. There are many marriage *motifs* in the dances; they were written in the 'finest frenzy' in my experience. Some day I will explain them to you.

. . . And now, after writing to you on six happy days in succession, I must return to quietness, loneliness, darkness. . . .

73.

Robert to Clara.

LEIPZIG, *February* 6, 1838.

. . . All the papers are full of you, as I expected. I go to the museum every day and read the Vienna notices. You say I do not realize what you are as an artist, and you are partly right, partly quite wrong. You may have strengthened your individuality, reached a higher stage of perfection, but I know my dear enthusiastic girl so well of old that I could tell her playing miles away. Grillparzer's poem[1] is the finest thing that has ever been written about you. I realized afresh the divine nature of the poet's art, which can say the right thing in so few words and for all time. Mendelssohn happened to be with me when I received it, and he said the same. 'A shepherd maiden,' 'the touch of her white fingers as she played'—what delicate language this is! It gives a living picture of you. These few lines will be worth more to you from the public point of view than all Wiest's[2] articles, for even the common people look upon a poet with awe, . . . accept his dictum and venture no contradiction. In short, the poem has given me great pleasure; and if your lover, or, indeed, any lover, could write poems, he could not do anything better than this. I am sorry to hear, however, that it is being set to music. That is unpoetical, and spoils the whole effect. A real composer would never have done it, though a girl like you might well tempt one to sin against his conscience. But you would restore him to virtue by your own, my Clara—that virtue which has brought me back to life, and is a perpetual inspiration to greater purity. I was a poor, beaten wretch, who for eighteen

[1] See introduction to this section.

[2] A Vienna journalist.

months could neither pray nor weep, for eye and heart were cold and hard as iron. And now, what a change! Your love and loyalty have made me a new creature. . . . I sometimes feel as if my heart were crossed by a thousand narrow intersecting paths, along which my thoughts and feelings race up and down, and in and out, like human beings, asking, Whither does this way lead? and that? and all the ways? And the answer is always the same: 'to Clara.' . . .

Have you not received the *Davidstänze?* . . . I sent them to you a week last Saturday. You will, I know, make a little place in your heart for them, because they are mine. . . . But my Clara will know how to find the real meaning of those dances, for they are dedicated to her in a quite special sense. The whole thing represents a *Polterabend*,[1] and I leave you to fill in the beginning and the end yourself. I never spent happier moments at the piano than in composing these. . . .

And now I have something to ask of you. Will you not pay a visit to our beloved Schubert and Beethoven? Take with you some sprigs of myrtle, twine them together in twos, and lay them on the graves, if you can. Whisper your name and mine as you do it—not a word besides. You understand? . . .

[1] The evening before the wedding, when there is a party given up to games and romps. [Tr.]

74.

Robert to Clara.

LEIPZIG, *February* 11, 1838.

Come and sit beside me, my dear, sweet girl. Hold your head a little to the right, in the charming way you have, and let me talk to you a little.

I have hardly ever been so happy as just lately. It must give you some pleasure to feel that you have brought back to life and happiness a creature who was for years a prey to the most terrifying thoughts, and had a positive genius for seeing the dark side of everything, so that he trembles as he looks back on a time when he did not value his life at a brass farthing. (I am going to lay bare my inmost soul to you, as I never did to living being. You, my dearest on earth, shall know all.)

My real life begins at the point when I arrived at a clear conception of myself and my talent, and by choosing art marked out a definite course for my energies. This was in 1830. You were then a queer little girl, with strong views of your own, beautiful eyes, and a weakness for cherries. I had no one else but my dear Rosalie.[1] A few years passed. As early as 1833 a certain melancholy made itself felt, of which I obstinately refused to take any account, regarding it merely as the disheartenment experienced by every artist when results are not achieved with the speed he expected. I received small recognition; moreover, I lost the use

[1] His sister-in-law, who died in 1833.

of my right hand for playing. But in the midst of all these dark thoughts and visions you haunted me at every turn. You have, indeed, though without conscious will or knowledge, kept me these many years from all intercourse with other women. The first glimmering of the idea that you might one day be my wife occurred to me even then, but it all lay in the too distant future. However, I loved you even in those earliest days with all the affection possible, considering our years. My love for Rosalie, whom I can never forget, was very different. We were of the same age. She was more than a sister to me, but, of course, actual love was out of the question. She looked after me, gave me good advice, encouraged me, and expected great things of me, and so I loved to think of her image. This was in the summer of 1833. But I was very seldom happy, for I felt the lack of something. The death of a dear brother threw me into a state of melancholy, which gained more and more the upper hand. The news of Rosalie's death found me in this condition. I won't say much about it. In the night between the 17th and 18th of October I was seized with the worst fear a man can have, the worst punishment Heaven can inflict—the fear of losing one's reason. It took so strong a hold of me that consolation and prayer, defiance and derision, were equally powerless to subdue it. Terror drove me from place to place. My breath failed me as I pictured my brain paralyzed. Ah, Clara! no one knows the suffering, the sickness, the despair, except those so crushed. In my terrible agitation I went to a doctor and told him everything—how my senses often failed me so that I did not know which way to turn in my fright, how I could not be certain of not taking my own life when in this helpless condition. And now, my angel from heaven, I must tell you that the doctor, after comforting me kindly, told me that medicine was useless, and ended by advising marriage as the only cure. I felt much relieved, for it seemed possible. At that time you were just between childhood and girlhood, and took little notice of me. Just then Ernestine came on the scene—as good a girl as the world holds. She, I thought, was the one to rescue me. I longed to cling to some womanly heart. I grew better. She loved me, as I could see. Well, you know all about it—the parting, our correspondence, our intimacy. That was in the winter of 1834. But, once she was away, and I began to think out what it might lead to, the whole affair began to weigh heavily. I heard how poor she was. I knew how little I could earn, for all my efforts, and could see no way out at all. Then I heard of the unfortunate family complications in which she was mixed up, and confess I was hurt at her silence to me on the subject.

You will blame me, but I must admit that the sum of these things cooled my attachment. My career as an artist seemed madness. The vision to which I had clung for salvation now haunted my dreams as a ghost. I saw myself condemned to work for my bread like a day-labourer. Ernestine was incapable of earning anything. I talked it over with my mother, and we both agreed that it could only add new cares to those already existing.

75.

Robert to Clara.

LEIPZIG, *March* 17, 1838.

How shall I begin to tell you what a different creature you are making of me, you dear, splendid person! Your letter led me from one heaven to another. What a new life, what glorious prospects, you open up to me! Sometimes as I go through your letters I feel like the first man, as he was led by an angel through the whole new creation; as they go from height to height, where each new prospect is fairer than the last, the angel says: 'All this is thine.' Is all this really mine? Do you know that it is a long-cherished wish of mine to spend some years in the city the beauties of which undoubtedly helped to inspire two great men in the noblest artistic production, the city of Beethoven and Schubert? All that you tell me in your true and loving letter strengthens my wish to come at once. . . .

. . . It is settled, then? Your hand on it! Our goal is Vienna. All my convictions, all my wishes, point to it. We shall leave some things behind . . . our mother-country, our families, and, lastly, Leipzig, which is quite a respectable town after all. The parting from Theresa and my brothers will be hard. I shall also miss my native soil, for I love this patch of earth, and am a Saxon, body and soul. You too are a Saxon, and will have to tear yourself from father and brothers. Joy and sadness will be mingled in our wedding chimes, but we will listen to the joyous ones. You will lean on my heart—happy heart! IT IS SETTLED. WE GO.

. . . We have only your father's love and respect to win. How gladly would I call him father, to whom I owe so much in joy, in knowledge—and in sorrow. I wish him nothing but happiness in his old age. . . . If he had known me better he might have spared me much grief and that letter which took two years off my life. But I have suffered, and forgiven him. He is your father; he has brought you up to be the noblest of your sex, and only tries to weigh your welfare to assure himself of your perfect happiness and safety, even as he has always protected you. I cannot remonstrate with him, for I am convinced he only seeks your good.

Saturday afternoon.

. . . I have discovered that suspense and longing are the best spurs to the imagination. I have had my full share of these the last few days, as I sat waiting for your letter and writing whole volumes of wonderful, crazy, gay compositions, which will make you open your eyes when you play them. Indeed, I sometimes feel as if I should burst with music. Before I forget, let me tell you what I have written. Whether or no in response to some words you once wrote saying I sometimes seemed to you like a child, I took flight and amused myself with working out thirty droll little pieces, twelve of which I have selected and christened *Kinderszenen*. You will like them, though you will have to forget you are a virtuoso for the time being. They bear inscriptions such as 'Bogeys,' 'By the Fireside,' 'Blindman's-buff,' 'A Child's Petition,' 'Hobby-horseman,' 'From Foreign Lands,' 'An Uncanny Story,' and what not. They are descriptive enough, you see, and as easy as winking. . . . I wonder how we shall find ourselves situated in the summer. I am prepared to adopt a reasonable attitude, but my old friendly footing in your family is impossible. We shall never feel comfortable until your father recognizes me as a future son of the house; even a passive recognition would be better than none, and need commit him to nothing. He should never have cause to regret it. I would do anything to please him then. But did his words only arise from a wish to cheer you in Vienna? Is it possible he may forget all he said? You are such a dear, sweet girl; next time the subject comes up, hold him to his promise so that he cannot slip out of it later. Fall on his neck and say: 'Dear father, be kind and bring him with you sometimes, for he really cannot live without me.'

The more I think of our life in Vienna, the more delightful it seems. With such a housekeeper to order my house, such a wife to reign in my heart—a beloved and loving wife in whom the world honours a rare artist—with means to live, youth to enjoy the honourable career which lies before me in this new country, who would not be happy? Beautiful scenery, pleasant society and associations, work to keep us occupied and content, and the many interesting connexions we shall form in such a centre, are all so many added attractions. Your father *must* say yes. It would be a sin if he refused.

. . . My life, for these three months past, has been very quiet, the most startling contrast to yours; but, indeed, yours would stun me, were I in your place. I rise early, usually before six, and this first hour is the most precious of my whole day. My room is transformed into a chapel, with the piano for an organ and your picture for the altar-piece. . . .

. . . What shall you call yourself, by the way? Wieck-Schumann, or the other way round, or just Clara Schumann? How charming and natural that looks!

Monday, March 19.

My darling girl, if I could but find one word to sum up everything you are to me! But there is none. Do I not adore you—let me say it!—as if you were divine; do I not know your heart and my own? What a joy your music will be to me, too! If I once said I only loved you because of your goodness, it was only half true. Everything is so harmoniously combined in your nature that I cannot think of you apart from your music—and so I love the one with the other. . . .

76.

Robert to Clara.

LEIPZIG, *April* 14, 1838.
Saturday before Easter.

. . . I am but human, and I am often conscious of hating him with a bitter hatred, which is strangely out of keeping with the love I bear his daughter. But he will go back on his word repeatedly, as he has done before, and I see plainly that we cannot count on him, but must *act for ourselves.* Listen then, Clärchen. I propose to go to Vienna as soon as possible. I only want your consent. Ever since I made up my mind, and realized the beauty of your plan, I have been consumed with impatience. . . . Now I want you to satisfy me on one important point. Putting aside the question of your father's consent, will you give me an approximate date for our marriage? I think if we fixed Easter, 1840, over two years from now, you would have proved yourself the most dutiful of children, and could leave your father with a clear conscience, even should he protest with violence. We shall be of age; and you will have deferred to your father's desire that you should wait another two years. There can be no question of testing our loyalty; I will never let you go . . . your hand upon it! *In two years' time* is our watchword! . . .

Sunday morning.

. . . I am half inclined to give up the idea of seeing you this summer. If I have survived without it two years, two more of the same penance will not kill me. What satisfaction is there in the few disjointed words we should steal at odd moments, in fear and trembling? I want you for always—days, years, eternities. I have done with quixotic notions. Of course I will come if you want it very much, but otherwise let us give it up as useless. . . . I want you for my wife. This is my earnest, sacred wish; to all else I am indifferent.

77.

Robert to Clara.

LEIPZIG, *May* 10, 1838.

. . . So your father calls me phlegmatic? Phlegmatic, and write the *Carnaval*, the F sharp minor sonata! Phlegmatic, and your lover! And you can listen to this calmly? He accuses me of having written nothing in the paper for six weeks. That is, first of all, untrue, and in the second place, were it true, he knows what other work I have been doing. Besides, where is the material to come from every time? Up to now I have provided close upon eighty printed sheets of original matter for the paper, not counting the rest of my editorial work. I have also completed ten considerable compositions within these two years. There is heart's blood in them, too! I give several hours daily to the serious study of Bach and Beethoven, outside my own studies. I carry on a large and often complicated correspondence methodically. I stay quietly at home in Saxony, in spite of my twenty-eight years and my quick-stirring artist's pulse. I save money, and spend nothing on feasting or betting, but take my peaceful walk to Gohlis, as of old, for sole recreation. But your father makes no account of my diligence and sobriety or of the work I do. . . . One would like to be modest, but the world will not let us, and so, for once, you see, I praise myself. You know now what to think of me and what to expect. . . .

78.

Robert to Clara.

September 9, 1838.

It is still a dream to me, all that I listened to yesterday, all that went on around me.[1] I was divided between rage and delight. I had chosen a nice dark corner, to avoid meeting anyone's eyes. You probably could not see me either, much as I should have wished it. I saw you the whole time, and the ring gleaming on the second finger of your left hand. Come and let me kiss you again and again for the way you played to me yesterday—you, my own Clara, with your beautiful soul and

[1] Clara had given a concert at the Gewandhaus, Leipzig.

your wonderful talent! You played magnificently! People don't half deserve what you give them. As you sat there all alone, supreme in the mastery of your art, and people spoke of you as if it were all a matter of course, I thought how happy I was to call such a treasure my own, and also felt very strongly that I could dispense with the crowd who were there simply to say they had heard you. You are too dear, too noble, for the career which is to your father the aim, the crown, of existence. Are these few hours worth so much expenditure of time and energy? Can you look forward to a continuation of this as your whole vocation? No; my Clara is to be a happy wife, a contented, beloved wife! Indeed, I reverence your art, and dare hardly think of all the happiness promised me in connexion with it; but, unless we are really in want, you shall not touch a note to please people for whom scales are too good—unless you wish it. Does my dear girl understand me? As an artist, I consider that you can serve art without long concert tours, and my musical soul will not be critical if you hurry here, pause there, in your playing, or put a finer finish on to anything, so long as the inspiration is there, as in your case it is. . . . I had so much more to tell you to-day, but I am too excited. I shall go to sleep and dream of nothing but you.

Good-bye, my best, best-beloved, my heart's treasure, my own dearest Clara! Yours, and yours only.

79.

Robert to Clara.

VIENNA,
Sunday morning, October 7, 1838.

Give you greeting, my dearest girl, from our new home—no home to me as yet, alas! for you are not here. By Friday night I felt as homesick and depressed as any exile. . . . I turned over many things in my mind. . . . Then Doppler brought me a letter addressed in an unknown hand. I opened it, and found it was from your father, quite in the tone of Kotzebue. I will copy it for you. . . .

I was pining to hear from you, and went to the post. But there was nothing, and I had to go sadly home again. Then, who should come but Fischhof's mother with your letter! What can I possibly reply? I am so far away, and so many terrible things may happen while letters are on the way. You are my only hope. You have always shown so much courage that nothing which may come will dismay you. . . . So now, listen. If your father insists on your departure, go. I can well imagine your inward struggle between gratitude to your father and devotion to me, but you must take comfort in remembering that you have done all that can be expected of a daughter, and tried every gentle and loving art to gain your end. Think how many girls (some of gentle birth) have been forced to take the step to which your father is driving you. *Our time has come.* Perhaps you have realized it, and taken prompt action. You admit, in so many words, that he will never consent, that you must wrench yourself free; let it be now, then, as soon as possible. Seize the first opportunity. This state of things is undermining your health, and must not go on. You have some duties towards yourself. Leave Leipzig now—any day—to-morrow! Where can you go? My poor, long-suffering Clara, lift your eyes to mine. Where, indeed! You cannot come to me yet, but you can be on the way. Serre or Theresa will take you in. . . . Your most daring move would be to go to Theresa, as it would certainly hasten matters. But more of this later. . . .

. . . If you feel equal to Paris, and can be sure of earning enough, spend the winter there by all means. *My confidence in you is boundless.* Do what seems to you the easiest.

And now, my dear Clara, you will need money in either case. I am writing by this post to Dr. Günz at Leipzig, who will give you a thousand gulden whenever you ask him. He knows pretty well everything about us. I shall always remember the way in which he said, as we parted: 'Count on me unreservedly; I will do anything for you and Clara.' So do not hesitate to ask for what you need, my darling. The money is better in your hands than in mine. . . .

80.

Robert to Clara.

December 3, 1838.

Thalberg[1] lives a long way from me. We have not met for a month, but I shall see him this evening at Dessauer's. He leaves for Leipzig to-morrow on his way to Berlin and other places. He played beautifully at his concerts, but his compositions certainly lack vitality. I confess that to me, and to many others here, you are worth ten of him. My lame hand makes me wretched sometimes—here especially. It grows worse, too, as I don't mind admitting to you. I often bemoan my fate, and demand to know why Heaven should send me this particular trial. It would mean so much here if I were able to play. What a relief to give utterance to all the music surging within me! As it is, I can barely play at all, but stumble along with my fingers all mixed up in a terrible way. It causes me great distress.

Well, I have you for my right hand. Take care that nothing happens to you. I often think of the happy hours I shall spend listening to you. Are you still working as hard as ever? I know you are. The satisfaction which the knowledge of your own power affords you may be even keener when you have a constant listener able to appre-

[1] Sigismund Thalberg (1812-1871), Liszt's rival in the public favour as a pianist.

ciate you and follow your every mood. Have you been writing and composing lately?

. . . Let me give you one piece of advice: *don't improvise too much.* It is such a waste of precious material. Make a point of writing everything down; you will thus collect and concentrate your ideas. You are denied the tranquillity and security from interruption which are the essential conditions for finishing a composition perfectly. But time may one day bring you these. . . .

I have composed very little here; I seem to have lost the art. But I have been through that stage before, and know that I shall work all the better after it. You may be sure that I shall not let Vienna spoil me.

81.

From Schumann's Verses to Clara.

VIENNA, 1838.

(These verses were elegantly written on four slips of paper, fastened together and decorated with dainty designs.)

I.

A maid of twenty and not yet a wife,
A man of thirty who is but a lover,
Are losing fast, and never may recover,
The Spring of life.

* * *

Laurel's a crown for the artist's prize,
And thine own are the bays that thou wearest;
But, for the garland a maiden ties
For her hair, 'tis the myrtle that's fairest.

* * *

There is a bride, a faithful bride, for me,
And in her eyes, for any man to see,
Is a sure gage of women's loyalty.

* * *

Truth hath never ruth.

* * *

Clärchen was Egmont's beloved—the same . . .
O the strange sweetness of the name!

* * *

Clärchen . . . Schumann . . . I wonder whether
An angel imagined the names together?

* * *

Parted we are,
Even as in the heavens star and star,
One following the other on its way,
Night and day.

* * *

Seek far and wide
Ere you will find two lovers such as these!
To vex me with unkindness once she tried—
She did but please.

* * *

She lingers still—
She will not give me all my happiness.
A brighter crown of myrtle will redress
The long ordeal.

* * *

Yet, not too long!
I could not bear for ever thus to wait;
The heart grows old, the will is less than strong,
The flames abate.

* * *

II.

If angrily Florestan scold thee,
Eusebius' arms shall enfold thee.

* * *

In Florestan are jealousies,
Eusebius loves thee trustfully—
So which shall have thy bridal kiss?
The truest to himself and thee.

* * *

But if thou wouldst be a masterful wife,
Then with two, not with one, will be the strife.
And who will win, then?
And who give in, then?

* * *

So we lead thee to thy throne, and we stand,
Right and left of thee, on either hand;
And if one of us offends thee and is banned,
Wilt thou banish both from thy land?

* * *

III.

Gladly and often have I let thee see
My inmost self, and from thine eye have guessed
Thou wert content; yet surely what was best
Therein, reflected thee.

* * *

But I unveiled not all. Thou wouldst have seen
Dark shapes of fear,
Deep sullen thoughts—ask me not what they mean . . .
Believe me, Dear.

* * *

If on thy heart and circled by thine arms I lay,
Wouldst thou not say
A true man is the masterpiece the inmost mind
Of God designed?

* * *

IV.

Years ago, when you were only a bright
Little maiden, they sent you to bed,
And I stood at your door in the failing light
Dressed as a bogey to give you a fright,
And you shrieked and you fled.
Ah, could I but see you disguised as then,
Would you not quickly discover,
And whisper so gently, ''Tis you, of all men!
Come, let me kiss you, and kiss you again. . . .
Do you like masquerading, my lover?'

* * *

'Wretched man! let them die;
These were childish follies.' 'Why?
Let those blissful hours pass by
Once again in memory.'

* * *

V.

'Together to live, to die,'
Was my farewell when last we said good-bye;
For parting showed, my life could not be lived
Were it of thine deprived.
Thou gavest me but a look, no word, but I
Read the bright answer of thy loyalty—
'Together to live, to die.'

* * *

Yea, when thou comest to die,
Through the dark earth I'll bear thee company;
So, with this sin upon me, I shall fare
To meet the happy spirits, and perchance
With thee, in thy perfected radiance,
Shall have a welcome there.

82.

Robert to Clara.

VIENNA,
Wednesday, December 18, 1838.

Give you greeting, my darling girl. You have created an atmosphere of spring; I can see golden blossoms peeping forth all around me. In other words, your letters started me on composing, and I feel as if I should never stop. Here is my little

Christmas gift.[1] You will grasp its significance. Do you remember Christmas Eve three years ago, and how passionately you embraced me? You seemed to be almost frightened at the way in which you let yourself go sometimes. It is different now, for you are assured of my love and know me through and through. My own love, my faithful companion, my wife! You will embrace me in quite another way two years hence, when I display your Christmas presents: a cap, various toys, and some new compositions. 'How lucky I am to have such a very good husband!' you will exclaim again and again, while I try in vain to moderate your transports. Then you will take me into your own room and show me mine: a miniature of yourself, a writing-board for composing, a sugar slipper—which I shall eat on the spot—and much besides, for you will outdo me in generosity. Don't I know you of old! Then, as we become quieter and the candles on the tree burn fainter, our kisses will breathe the prayer that time may make no change, but keep us united to the end.

My festival will be a sad one this year. I shall hum many a melody, and go to the window every now and then to look up at the glittering stars. In spirit I shall spend the whole evening with you.

. . . Would this happy mood might last! . . . But my strength always fails me when I am left long without a sign from you. Depression sets

[1] See *Bunte Blätter*, Op. 99, No. 1: 'A greeting to my betrothed on Christmas Eve, 1838.'

in, and I feel as if I were being swathed in endless black fabrics and garments, and stowed away—an indescribable sensation. . . .

83.

Robert to Clara.

VIENNA, *December* 29, 1838.

. . . I feel I should like to talk to you about certain of my phases. People are often at a loss to understand me, and no wonder! I meet affectionate advances with icy reserve, and often wound and repel those who really wish to help me. I have often taken myself to task about it. It is not that I fail to appreciate the very smallest attention, or to distinguish every subtle change in expression or attitude; it is a fatal something in my words and manner which belies me. But you will take me as I am, and make excuse, I know. My heart is in the right place, and my whole soul is responsive to the good and the beautiful. But enough of this. It is when I think of the future that I feel we ought to open our hearts to each other as unreservedly as children who practise no concealment. . . . I am reported to have said at Prague: 'I could write a Mozart G minor symphony in my sleep.' Some liar invented that. You know the modesty with which I approach all the great masters.

84.

Robert to Clara.

January 15, 1839.

My dearest Girl,

I can hardly tell you how your letter inspired me. How can I be worthy of you! I thought I had achieved the hardest task in leaving Leipzig: and now you, a young and tender girl, are braving the dangers of the great world for my sake. It is the noblest thing you ever did for me. I feel sure it means the end of our difficulties, too. You have put new strength into me. Some day your courage and independence will meet their reward. You are really a wonderful girl; no praise could be too great for you. And yet, when I awake in the night, to hear wind and rain beating on my window, and picture you on your journey, alone but for your art, with perhaps a glorious vision of the future to console you, then a flood of tenderness fills me, and I wonder what I have done to deserve so much love. You have transformed me, as I said before. It must be patent to all eyes. . . . It gives me *moral* strength to see my dear girl so brave. I have done as much work in these few days as I usually spread over weeks. It is like the time when we pledged our word, in August, 1837: work is a pleasure, success crowns every effort. See what you do to me, Clara! But it is natural that a heroic maiden like yourself should make her lover a little hero in his turn. . . . I wish I could follow you invisibly (if not visibly!), sheltering you under my wing, like a guardian angel, against all harm. Ah, Clara, how infinitely our love gains by work and sacrifice! . . .

85.

Robert to Clara.

LEIPZIG, *April* 10, 1839.

MY OWN BELOVED,

Our dear Eduard is dead.[1] When I was travelling, last Saturday, I distinctly heard, at half-past two in the morning, a chorale played on trombones. It was at that moment he died. I am still half-dazed after my exertions, and can find nothing to say. I was so looking forward to seeing my brothers, Theresa, and my friends here, and now comes this shadow. I dare not guess what else fate may have in store. Possibly these trials are so many steps towards happiness, and are intended to strengthen my character and make a man of me. Eduard was my only stand-by in trouble. He was so true to his word. We never had the smallest disagreement. His last words as I left him were: 'You are sure to succeed, you are such a good fellow.' But there was something in his eyes then which I can only call the death-look. None of our former partings had been so affectionate. I was also struck by his second, apparently motiveless visit to Leipzig. It was certainly ordained that he

[1] April 6.

should see us together that once. We were strolling along the promenade—you remember?—and I said, 'Well, Eduard, what do you think of us?' I know how proud he was that you loved me, and were one day to take the family name. Many sad recollections occur to me, but I shall have, all my life, the precious consciousness that I was always a good brother to him, even as he was to me. Nothing can be more perfect than the bond between two brothers. It no longer exists for me, alas! But you shall see; I will not let this trouble overwhelm me. . . .

86.

Robert to Clara.

LEIPZIG,
Saturday morning, May 4, 1839.

MY HEART'S DEAREST (so soon to be my wife)!

I spent yesterday morning with Reuter, making careful calculations, and came to the conclusion that we have been making mountains out of molehills. There is nothing to prevent our being married to-morrow if you, you obstinate little person, were willing. . . .

Our wealth seems to me quite terrific when I compare it with that of some people. How fortunate we are not to be obliged to work for our daily bread! There is just enough for two artists with simple tastes like ourselves. The idea makes me so happy.

Your capital ...	... ...	4,000 talers.
My capital:	1. Government stock ...	1,000 „
	2. With Karl	4,000 „
	3. With Eduard ...	3,540 „
	4. From Eduard's estate	1,500 „
		14,040 talers.
Interest	... ...	560 talers.
Other sources of yearly income:		
From Friese[1]	... ...	624 talers.
Sale of music	... ...	100 „
From compositions ...	...	100 „
Total yearly income	...	1,384 talers.

Am I not a famous arithmetician! . . . Supposing I were to insist, could you refuse to come to me now?

And is there not a margin left for an occasional bottle of champagne, or a little present to Theresa, should she need it, or to your mother? You see, you need not worry any more, my Clärchen. I am quite as cautious as you; I know the value of money, if anyone does. I assure you I have sometimes to guard against miserliness.

87.

Robert to Clara.

May 18, 1839.

It is raining and blowing a hurricane outside, but in my heart there is sunshine and a wonderful all-embracing love. Dear Clärchen, I want you here,

[1] The publisher of the *Zeitschrift für Musik.* [Tr.]

I want you to look into my heart. I confess I was ready to put an end to myself with all possible speed a few days ago,[1] but I decided to wait for your next letters. You reminded me strongly of a girl I think I once loved. It even seemed as if she still loved me, as if, indeed, she had never loved me more truly, and that, however impulsive and hasty she might be, she could not belie her own sweet nature. Gradually I came to feel more at home—first with the girl, whose beautiful forehead and cheeks I dared to stroke, then with myself in my anger at having to be so angry. Then other thoughts crept in. . . . I dreamed of Whitsuntide next year, saw myself a happy father, and, before that, a bridegroom, and so on. . . . And now it is Whitsun Eve, which always brings me a vision of the dove with the olive-branch, emblem of this lovely festival of spring and peace. So let me kiss you, my own first love. To think that I have

[1] Clara had written from Paris on May 5, 1839, suggesting that they should wait until their future was better assured, and so appease Wieck. Emilia List, with whom Clara was staying, wrote in the same strain, pointing out that Clara could not follow her artistic career unless she was rich enough to be independent of household cares. Emilia even proposed that Schumann should take over the book-shop of his brother Eduard as the readiest means of procuring the required income. These letters crossed with Schumann's enthusiastic epistle of May 4, and were followed by another still more discouraging letter from Clara, which Schumann immediately destroyed. Later he removed the traces of the misunderstanding by the destruction of his own answers, but some idea of his not unnatural resentment may be gathered from this letter of reconciliation. [Tr.]

you again, to know that your indecision has left you! How roughly I had to talk to you in my last letters; and yet, could you expect anything different? Ask yourself, put yourself in my place. It was your second letter which hurt me most. If you read it at some future time, you will deny your own words. Everything seemed to fall on me at once. Your father has again been most insulting. . . . From my friends, from Theresa, who was here for a few days—from everybody, without exception, I had to hear things which chafed my sense of honour unbearably. They all insisted that I had been abominably treated throughout, that you could not possibly have any great love for me if you were content to let it go on. On the top of this came your second letter, cold as the grave, discontented, perverse. My letter to Emilia was the result. I could not help taking that tone, cruelly as it hurt me. Those were terrible days. Every fibre of my being is affected by a mental upheaval such as this. . . . Where you are concerned my faculties are all doubly active, and it penetrates immediately to my very marrow. Was it [not] natural for me to write and act as I did, even though it pained you? Let this warn you, my dear Clara, to be very considerate in your treatment of me in the future. So much depends on the *form* of expression. You might have conveyed the same meaning in more measured language. As it was, you wrote at the pitch of excitement, while I was so unprepared for this sudden outburst that I doubted your constancy, so changed did you seem. And so I opened your next letter in trembling, but as I read on and on it was as if all heaven's gates opened to me in turn, for I knew you were mine again. . . . Ah, my dear Clara, is it possible that you are really coming to me next spring as my beloved wife? . . .

. . . Promise me you will never again give way to fears for our future. Promise to give up all useless worries, to trust and obey me, for the man is the head of the woman.

And you two other dear girls,[1] I was rather rude to you. May I hope for forgiveness? If I could join you now . . . what a festival of joy and peace we would celebrate. It would rain kisses. But you must not blame me for showing that I am master, and will not be trifled with. I am as easily led as a child, but I refuse to be driven. . . .

Listen, my Clärchen, our plan of waiting until Christmas before writing to your father is no good. We must do it sooner. . . . I therefore enclose two documents. The one addressed to your father I propose to send a few days before your birthday; the other we shall present to the court without delay in the case of your father's refusal. . . .

There is no other way of deciding the matter. I cannot impress it upon you too strongly, my dear Clara. . . .

[1] The List sisters.

. . . One thing more, my Clara, that you may be sure of me on every point. You have sometimes asked whether the financial cares of everyday life would not overwhelm me. In the first place, we need have no cares; but should this be the case, I would meet them smiling, even with the half of what we have. To have debts which I was unable to pay would harass me, but nothing else. I am too much of an idealist. But you must not jump to the conclusion that I am imprudent; have I not shown that I can be parsimonious—for your sake? . . .

Schumann's Letter to Friedrich Wieck.[1]

Once more I ask you, in Clara's name and my own, to give your consent to our union next Easter. Two years have passed since my first appeal. You doubted our constancy; but it has stood the test, and our confidence in a happy future is unshaken.

My former statement as to my means was exact. They are now better and more assured, and we can face the future fearlessly. Oh, be moved by the ties of nature! Do not drive us to extremes. Clara's twentieth birthday is close at hand. Give your consent, and make it a day of peace. Give us rest after our hard fight. You owe it to your-

[1] Enclosed in the above letter of May 18, although it was only to be presented in September. [Tr.]

self, to Clara, and to me. I shall await your final decision anxiously.

As of old, yours in affection and confidence,

R. SCHUMANN.

Dear Clara, the letter is cold, but one might as well try to be affectionate towards a block of ice. It is the best I can do. Tell me what you think of it. Hermann[1] is responsible for the greater part of the following letter :

We, the undersigned, have long entertained a strong mutual desire to be united in matrimony. There is an obstacle in our path which prevents the fulfilment of our desire. We are therefore, to our great regret, driven to seek this means of removing it. The father of the undersigned Clara Wieck persists in withholding his consent, despite our repeated requests. We are at a loss to understand the grounds of his refusal. We have not consciously offended in any way. Our financial position ensures freedom from anxiety. Herr Wieck's objection can only be due to a personal hostility to the undersigned, who, for his part, is under the impression that he amply fulfilled his obligations to his future wife's father. In any case, we are not inclined to go back on our carefully weighed resolution. We therefore present our petition as follows :

[1] An assessor, a friend of Schumann's.

Will the High Court cause Herr Wieck to give his paternal consent to our marriage, or, failing that, substitute legal permission? Only the imperative need for action reconciles us to this step. We seek our consolation in the hope that this painful breach, like many another, may be healed by time.

ROBERT SCHUMANN.

CLARA WIECK (*at this time in Paris*).

LEIPZIG, *September*, 1839.

For the first time you are called upon to unite your signature with mine, my dearest girl. How bitter-sweet it is! Please go carefully through the document, word by word. . . . You need not produce your birth certificate until the ceremony. The world is quite a tolerable place with you in it, dearest. . . . Remember me to Emilia and Henrietta. Tell them they must like me as much as I like them. Let Henrietta whisper you her happy word of encouragement: 'Press on to the goal.' Well, it will soon be settled. I believe in you again, absolutely. Write soon, my dear one.

88.

Robert to Clara.

LEIPZIG, *June 3*, 1839.

MY DEAR, DEAREST BRIDE,

This letter will reach you on my twenty-ninth birthday. May it find you in the best of health and spirits, and bring me to your mind more vividly than ever. . . . We can look back upon the past year with a clear conscience, for we have been faithful to each other and have succeeded in forwarding our great aim. The worst is over, I think, but we must still be wary, though near the haven. Fate has ordained that we should fight our way step by step; but when, one day, we stand at the altar, our 'yes' will be spoken with a conviction, an assured faith in our future happiness, that is quite without parallel. And do you know how I wish to fill up the intervening time? By making myself more worthy of you. This is no mere figure of speech. I am only proud with people who are arrogant without reason; real modesty, such as yours, makes me long to confess my weakness and to make myself better. I shall sometimes give you pain in the years to come, for my character is still unformed in some respects. I am far too restless, too childish at times, and too soft; too apt to indulge my fancies without considering other people. I have, in fact, my bad days, when there is nothing to be done with me. But your loving considerateness, which has stood so many tests, will be a constant stimulus. To be with you continually is, indeed, a liberal education. But these are mere words. Our love is, after all, the one certainty. You have, I believe, so wonderful a store in your heart that I need not fear to exhaust it. What amazes me, you dear girl, is your many-sidedness. How did you ever find time in your short life to cultivate all these fine qualities, especially in such surroundings? One thing I know, my gentle personality made an impression on you when you were very young. I think you would have been different but for knowing me. You will leave me this comforting assurance? I taught you to love, your father to hate—in the best sense of the word, for there are good haters. Under my influence you grew to be the ideal partner of my joys and sorrows. You were my best pupil, and have rewarded me by giving me yourself.

89.

Robert to Clara.

June 22, 1839.

With roses and acacias in full splendour, and you, my own love, in the full bloom of your loveliness, I am indeed the most favoured of mortals, overwhelmed with happiness, half smothered under the load of blossoms. You dear girl, I can really believe now that you love me in earnest. I wonder how you looked when you signed your name? Like Devrient in *Fidelio*, I imagine. Did not every part of you tremble except the hand, which grasped the pen firmly? Come and let me press you to my heart, you, my love, my everything. All this you have done for me; I can never hope to repay you. Let me kiss your brow, your eyelids, child, as I pray for your lasting happiness.

My courage has risen too; I have forgotten for the moment all our past troubles and worries. Our schooling has been unusually severe, but how well we have come to know each other! Are you as well satisfied with me as I with you? . . . Could I but show you to the world as you really are, Clara! You may have your peer among artists, but how many girls have your tenderness and firmness? Few indeed. . . .

. . . Your announcement of our engagement has rescued me from my false position. I thank you a thousand times! I should like to set a crown upon your head, but can only fall at your feet and look up to you with gratitude. In loving you, I love the best the world has to give. How much more could I say, were I not so closely bound to you! One clasp of your hand, to thank you for your whole-hearted trust in me, which is love's best gift.

Ever, ever your own loving

ROBERT.

90.

To Advocate Einert, Leipzig.

LEIPZIG, *June* 30, 1839.

DEAR SIR,

I should be glad if I could see you to-day on very important private business. As I may not be able to express myself with sufficient clearness and composure, however, I prefer to send you beforehand a strictly accurate statement in writing.

In September, 1837, I made a formal offer of marriage to Fräulein Clara Wieck through her father, Herr Friedrich Wieck, a dealer in musical instruments of this place. Our acquaintance was of long standing, and I had, before taking this step, exchanged a promise of marriage with her. Her father gave me no decisive answer until October of the same year, when he wrote expressing himself as directly opposed to our marriage on the ground of his daughter's small means and my own. I had in my first letter given him a truthful representation of my financial position, fixing my yearly income at about 1,300 talers.

Herr Wieck took his daughter to Vienna that winter, and Clara wrote to me from there in the spring of 1838 to say that her father had given his consent subject to certain conditions. On their return to Leipzig, Herr Wieck paid me a visit in my room without even referring to the matter. I was offended, and thereafter avoided him as much as possible. He, for his part, was irritated by my behaviour, and began openly to oppose our intended union, attempting in every possible way to lower me in the eyes of his daughter and others. With a view to relieving the strained situation, I went to Vienna in September, partly in the hope of mollifying Herr Wieck by my absence, partly to prepare a new existence for Clara and myself. But I found less scope than I had imagined, and returned in April of the present year. Meantime Clara's untiring efforts to win her father's consent were unavailing. He even went so far in his active hostility as to slander me in the most barefaced way. Clara, whose health had suffered by this unnatural behaviour, decided to travel, and went away without her father, though by no means without his consent. This was before my return to Leipzig. She is now in Paris. We began to see that we should never gain our point with Herr Wieck by peaceful methods, and were considering serious measures, when, some weeks ago, to our surprise, Clara received his written consent under certain conditions, which I now append. I hope they will not give you a false impression of me. The conditions were :

1. That we should not live in Saxony during his lifetime, but that I should undertake to earn as much elsewhere as I do through editing a musical paper here.

2. That he should keep Clara's money, paying 4 per cent. interest, and only paying over the capital five years hence.

3. That I should have the statement of my income, as submitted to him in September, 1837, legally vouched, and place it in the hands of a solicitor chosen by himself.

4. That I should make no attempt to communicate with him verbally or in writing until he so desires.

5. That Clara should give up all claim to inherit anything from him after his death.

6. That we should be married by Michaelmas.

We cannot submit to these conditions, the last excepted, and are therefore determined to have recourse to law.

To leave no stone unturned, I was prevailed

upon by Clara to write to him once more in a conciliatory tone. The answer, sent through his wife, was to the effect that he 'wished to have no further dealings with me.'

Yesterday I received from Paris the power of attorney, duly signed by Clara, and viséd by the Saxon embassy. I shall do myself the honour of showing it to you to-day, if possible, with the request that you will help the brave, faithful girl to the best of your power.

We want the matter settled with all possible dispatch, and are willing to make another peaceable attempt to secure our end if you advise it, and think there is anything to be gained by an interview with Herr Wieck. Failing that, we shall apply to the court, which cannot refuse its consent, as our income is assured.

But I can tell you the rest when I see you. Will you kindly fix a time for the interview, and send me word by the messenger? I ask your services in a noble cause, my dear sir—the reunion of two lovers who have been parted for many years. We look to you for help, and need hardly add a request for strictest secrecy.

May I claim your sympathy for my betrothed as for myself?

Yours faithfully,

ROBERT SCHUMANN,

Editor of the 'Neue Zeitschrift für Musik.'

c/o MLLE. DEVRIENT,
First Floor,
Rotes Kollegium Hinterhaus.

91.

To Advocate Einert.

[LEIPZIG], *July* 3, 1839.

DEAR SIR,

I must apologize for troubling you again, but the honour and happiness of two people are at stake—two people who really deserve to be united after the sufferings they have endured. I feel I must discuss the matter with you again, going over each point in detail. Please fix a time when I can see you. If you should have the smallest doubt of our ultimate success, do not hide it from me. Clara would be beside herself if this public attempt should fail, and how shall I describe my own feelings in such an event! Therefore, if you are doubtful, we must seek another solution, though I confess I know of none at present. If, on the other hand, you feel sure of our success, you must reassure me, and help my heroic girl with the devotion she deserves.

I can practically tell you beforehand Herr Wieck's objections to me. He will probably bring forward a prior attachment to a girl[1] who lived in his house. She loved me, and I was very fond of her, but there were difficulties in the way of our marriage with which I was unable to cope, and we separated by mutual consent in January, 1836. I may say that she is now married. The incident does not, therefore, affect the present situation.

[1] Ernestine von Fricken (see Letter 74). [Tr.]

If you should hear anything else from Herr Wieck concerning my private life, please remember that he is exceedingly slanderous and malignant. A certain amount of dissipation in the time before I knew Clara is all I have to reproach myself with. You will perhaps come to know me better yourself in time. I can think of no other accusation which the opposition could produce. It is principally a question of my means. I have given you the documents relating to this matter, and will only add that I have no debts, except the trifling domestic accounts, which usually run for a month, and do not amount to more than twenty talers.

I assure you Herr Wieck's hostility is due solely to the fact that our marriage would mean the collapse of certain financial speculations. I should not be surprised if he demanded compensation for the pianoforte-lessons he has given his daughter!

I should also be glad to know whether you think my share of my late brother's property (a good-sized bookshop with house, etc.) should be taken into consideration in the statement of my income; also whether I ought to obtain attestations, as I could in a short time, of minor sources of income, such as compositions and reviews of music sent to the paper, which amount to about 300 talers yearly at least. . . .

I cannot tell you, my dear sir, how wearing all this is; I can only beg you to forgive me for troubling you so often. My messenger will wait for your reply, telling me at what time to-day you can spare me half an hour. Trusting that you will give me your help and sympathy,

Yours faithfully,

R. SCHUMANN.

92.

Robert to Clara.

Tuesday, July 30, 1839.

MY DEAREST, DEAREST CLARA,

I must send to you, in your lonely, detached village,[1] a message from this place, where I am reminded so vividly of you by your mother.[2] I cannot help loving her for her eyes, which are so like yours. Indeed, I always find it difficult to tear myself away from her. I spent the whole day there yesterday, and even kissed her good night, which made me perfectly happy. Our talk was of you, and you only. . . . She received me so kindly and affectionately, and seemed really to like me. If only we had you with us! Yesterday evening, as we were walking in the Tiergarten, I was so sad to think of my lonely girl so far away, who little thought that her mother and her lover were talking of her here. . . .

Your mother intends writing to you to-day. . . .

[1] Clara had left Paris for Bougival with Henrietta List. [Tr.]

[2] Clara's mother, Marianne, *née* Tromlitz, had married Adolf Bargiel, professor of music in Berlin, after her divorce from Wieck.

So you are afraid your father may fetch you away again? But, Clara, my dear child, you must surely have means of defending yourself. I cannot think he will do it, but if he insists on your going back to him you must simply say: 'I will not. I am going to my mother.' He is then quite powerless.

As I told you in a letter, I brought your picture with me, and I wish you could have seen your mother's face when I showed it her. Her tears overflowed at once; she quite lost her composure. The Bargiel children exclaimed, as soon as they saw it: 'That is Clara!' How happy it made me to hear them. . . .

93.

Robert to Clara.

LEIPZIG, *December* 11, 1839.

. . . Oh, Clara, I have been in paradise to-day! They played at the rehearsal a symphony[1] of Franz Schubert's. How I wish you had been there, for I cannot describe it to you. The instruments all sing like remarkably intelligent human voices, and the scoring is worthy of Beethoven. Then the length, the divine length, of it! It is a whole four-volume novel, longer than the choral symphony. I was supremely happy, and had nothing left to wish for, except that you were my wife and that I could write such symphonies myself.

[1] In C major. [Tr.]

94.

Robert to Clara.

LEIPZIG, *February* 24, 1840.

. . . The beginning of your letter to-day brought me to such a pass again that I did not know what to do. Finally, I wrote to Rackemann[1] and warned him that if he allows this lampoon[2] to circulate he will be an agent in spreading a vile calumny, and I shall sue him. I sent the letter through Töpken, with the request to find me a legal adviser, if necessary. Our only chance in such cases is, as you see, dear Clara, to take prompt and stringent measures. Justice and honour demand it. . . . You know what Goethe says:

'When is honour gained? When maintained.'

Gathy told me of the incredible reports that have been spread about me, and your letter confirms his. I hardly know myself in these days. But I mean to defend myself as long as there is blood in my veins.

Here I am again, breaking my resolution and saying what I ought not; but I cannot help it. You tell me I am becoming a positive misanthrope. but you are mistaken. My heart still has its love, its music and its ideals; have no fear. But can you wonder if I break into lamentations just once,

[1] A music-teacher at Bremen, in league with Wieck.

[2] Wieck had written and circulated a pamphlet against Schumann.

considering my provocation? When I think of what I have borne, my patience seems to me superhuman. Anyone else in my place would have given in sooner. But you must know that I chose for my pattern—yourself, Clara. I know well that your burden is no whit less than my own. . . .

95.

Robert to Clara.

Wednesday, March 18, 1840.

Do not expect much of a letter this time, for I am tired out with all the excitement of the past few days. . . . As long as Liszt is here I cannot do much work, and do not know how I am going to be ready by Holy Thursday, for I am with him nearly all day. He said yesterday: 'I feel as if I had known you twenty years,' and I have just the same feeling towards him. We have arrived at the stage of being as rude as we like to each other, and I have frequent cause to avail myself of the privilege, as he is really too capricious and has been spoilt by his stay in Vienna. I shall not be able to squeeze into this letter all I have to tell you of our first meeting at Dresden, the concert, my railway journey back yesterday, last night's concert, and this morning's rehearsal for the next. I have at last had a chance of hearing Liszt's wonderful playing, which alternates between a fine frenzy and the utmost delicacy. But his world is not mine, Clärchen. Art, as we know it—you when you play, I when I compose—has an intimate charm that is worth more to me than all Liszt's splendour and tinsel! But enough for to-day. You understand all I would say.

96.

Robert to Clara.

LEIPZIG, *March* 20, 1840.

. . . I wish you could have been with Liszt this morning. He is really too extraordinary. His playing of the *Novelletten*, parts of the *Phantasie*, and the sonata, moved me strangely. Although his reading differed in many places from my own, it was always inspired, and he does not, I imagine, display such tenderness, such boldness, every day. Becker was the only other person present. I think he had tears in his eyes. The second *Novellette* in D gave me peculiar pleasure. You can hardly believe the effect it makes. Liszt is going to play it at his third concert here. But there have been complications too, so many that I should fill volumes were I to describe them to you. His second concert has been postponed, as he chose to go to bed, announcing, only two hours beforehand, that he was ill. I will gladly believe that he is, and was at the time, suffering from over-exertion, but all the same it was a politic illness. I cannot now go into it all. It suits me excellently, because I can keep him in bed all day, and have him all to myself, with Mendelssohn, Hiller and Reuss. No one else is admitted. If only you had been there

15

this morning, little girl, you would have been affected in the same way as Becker, I wager.

. . . Will you believe that at his concert he played on an instrument of Härtel's which he had never seen before? This unbounded confidence in his own ten fingers is just the sort of thing I like. But do not take pattern by him in this; be always my own Clara Wieck. No one can touch you, for your playing comes from your heart. Do you hear, child?

. . . A month to-day I shall be with you, God willing, dear child. Shall you not be happy to feel my arms about you again? Will you arrange a little private concert for your lover? I should like the big sonata in B flat (the whole of it), then one of my own songs, played and sung by yourself (the words are the chief thing, remember), then your new scherzo, and, to wind up, Bach's C sharp minor fugue from the second book. It is not to be a charity concert! I am prepared to pay liberally. We shall settle our accounts at the end—you can guess in what coin. How I shall look forward to this lovers' recital! You dearest, best of creatures, I shall smother you with kisses when I see you.

97.

Robert to Clara.

LEIPZIG, *May* 10, 1840.

To-day is 'Jubilate' Sunday, and I feel jubilant and wretched by turns over the happiness and misery which fall to my lot. But do not think of me as unhappy. I feel so well and brisk that I work almost without knowing it, and am so happy for thinking of you that I can't resist telling you. The opera[1] has taken up all my morning. The first sketch is finished, and I burn to begin, though I am nearly overwhelmed by the vastness of my material. It is very tragic at this point, though without bloodshed or the usual stage effects. I am quite enthusiastic—as I am sure you will be—over the characters which I am to recast in a musical mould. Yesterday I received a most delightful and opportune letter and article from Frau von Chezy about her collaboration with Weber in *Euryanthe*, together with his sketches, letters, notes, etc. Weber must have been one of the most refined and intellectual of musicians. The article will appear in the paper. I know you will be interested in it.

98.

Robert to Clara.

LEIPZIG, *May* 15, 1840.

I have been composing so much that I wonder at myself. But I cannot help it. I could sing myself to death, like a nightingale. I have finished the twelve Eichendorff songs,[2] and forgotten them

[1] From 1830 onward Schumann was occupied with plans for writing opera, but only *Genoveva* was performed.

[2] A song cycle (Op. 39), words by Eichendorff. [Tr.]

in the stress of beginning new work. My libretto is worrying me. J. Becker brought me a specimen the other day, which convinced me that he was not equal to his task. I have a horror of setting weak verses to music. It is not that I insist on a great poet, but I must have beauty of language and sentiment. Well, I shall certainly not give up my fine idea, for I feel I have dramatic talent. You will be amazed to see how the thing turns out. . . .

99.

Robert to Clara.

LEIPZIG, *May* 31, 1840.

. . . I am so impatient to see you and to have you tear me away from my music. You will be amazed to see the quantity of work I have finished in this short time. There is only the copying left to do. But it is high time I stopped, and I cannot. . . . Composing is making me forget how to write or think; my letters prove it. Oh, why did I not realize earlier that music was my sole vocation? You say in your last letter that you want me to fill my right place in the world. Don't be too ambitious for me. I want no better place than a seat at the piano with you close by. You will never be a Kapellmeisterin as long as you live, but in ourselves we shall be a match for any Kapellmeister and his wife, eh? . . . How little I thought when I published Op. 1 that I should ever reach Op. 22! Well, it is not so bad a record for eight years. I will do as much again, and then die. I sometimes feel I am striking quite new paths in music.

100.

To Ernst A. Becker.

LEIPZIG, *August* 12, 1840.

MY VERY DEAR FRIEND,

You must be the first to hear the glad news. Our suspense came to an end yesterday with the legal authorization to our marriage. You may be sure we shall take the next steps without delay. We are to be married in a village near here. Will you do us the pleasure of acting as witness? Clara's mother and aunt, and possibly my brother, will be the only people there. September 12 is to be the day which unites us. Promise me you will not mention the date to anyone, for one can never be sure the old man will not play us some scurvy trick. You must really come. We shall all be so happy together.

Clara is at Weimar, and played before the Empress yesterday. This may be very useful, as we shall perhaps go to St. Petersburg this winter.

Well, good-bye, old man. Remember us to all who are really interested. I hope soon to hear that you have decided to come.

* * * * *

From Clara's Diary.

September 12.—What can I write about this day? . . . We were married at Schönefeld[1] at ten o'clock. First came a chorale, and after that a short address by Wildenhahn, the preacher, a friend of Robert's youth. His words were simple, but heartfelt. My whole self was filled with gratitude to Him who had brought us safely over so many rocks and precipices to meet at last. I prayed fervently that He would preserve my Robert to me for many, many years. Indeed, the thought that I might one day lose him is enough to send me out of my mind. Heaven avert this calamity! I could not bear it.

Emilia and Elise List took me by surprise after the wedding. We spent the morning in company with Reuter, Wenzel, Herrmann, Becker, Mother and the Lists, at the Carls'; the afternoon at Zweinaundorf, and the evening at the Carls' again, when Madame List came too.

There was a little dancing, no excessive gaiety, but every face shone with real satisfaction. The weather was lovely. Even the sun, which had hidden his face for many days, shed his warm beams upon us as we drove to church, as if to bless our union. It was a day without a jar, and I may thus enter it in this book as the fairest and most momentous of my life.

[1] A village near Leipzig.

BOOK III

AT THE ZENITH (1840-1854)

'The man and the musician in me have always struggled to manifest themselves simultaneously; indeed, this is still the case, although I have attained some degree of mastery over both.'—*To* C. KOSSMALY, *May* 5, 1843.

'I am happy in the knowledge that greater achievements lie between me and the distant goal, of the attainment of which I am nevertheless confident.'—*From the Diary, September* 13, 1840.

'We are all pretty well; the melancholy birds of night still flit round me from time to time, yet they can be driven off by music.'—*To* VERHULST, *November* 4, 1848.

INTRODUCTION

SCHUMANN'S outer life during the years following his marriage was smooth and uneventful. His was a purely introspective nature, and when he sought to cope with external affairs he failed signally. His projects usually remained projects. His one considerable public undertaking—as a conductor at Düsseldorf—was a fiasco. So crude a dissonance should have been avoided at all costs. Blame probably attached to both sides, though allowance must be made for Schumann, whose sad fate had marked him before his friends suspected anything. Even in the early days of his marriage Schumann had complained of bats whirring around him; this illusion haunted him continually, and unfitted him for any public position. He carried out his high ideals in his teaching at the Leipzig Conservatorium (founded 1843), but was obliged by the state of his nerves to resign. Neither was he ever well when he accompanied his wife on concert tours.

His one idea of happiness was to sit at home and compose. The creative impulse dominated him. There were periods of unresting, even alarming, production, but this tropical fertility was invariably attended by the sultriness and oppression ever prophetic in Schumann's case of thunder and the devastating storm. The zealous worker broke down altogether, and waited in dull inaction for the next spring and autumn, for another blossoming and ripening of the fruits of his genius. Strangest of all, his powerful genius did always pull itself together for a new effort. The only suspicious symptom to the close observer was that his work was no longer quite up to his earlier level.

But the eyes which watched him most closely were full of love. The marriage of Robert Schumann with Clara Wieck is perhaps the most beautiful artist union we know. The development of the relation may be traced in Berthold Litzmann's biography (*Clara Schumann*, vol. ii.). We have there a moving and exquisite picture of Clara's transformation from virtuoso to artist as she became one with her husband, of her spiritual growth in the struggle to reconcile the claims of art with those of practical life. It was only when misfortune overtook her, when her happiness was wrecked, that her character showed its true greatness. The blow fell on February 27, 1854. They had been barely four years at Düsseldorf, for which they had so willingly exchanged Dresden, where the musical atmosphere was lacking. In point of fact they did not mind where they lived, provided they had each other and a home to work in.

The following letters will show how prolific in impressions, given and received, these years were for Schumann. It would have been easy to select twice or three times the number, but I have made it as small as possible. My aim is to show clearly the master's own development, from which an idea of his methods of work may be gained. The letters chosen are often typical of a series of similar ones, all valuable in themselves, and available in Jansen's collection, which, large as it is, is not complete.

101.

To Camille Stamaty,[1] *in Paris.*

LEIPZIG, *September* 28, 1840.

Your letter was the pleasantest surprise. How could you hear of the happy event so speedily? I would have sent you word myself, but was too absorbed in my happiness. I think you will understand, and forgive me. You know, too, how much of my time is taken up by official correspondence and various musical matters.

The years that have intervened since I last wrote have been extremely eventful. You will find many of my struggles reflected in my compositions. How I wish you knew the later ones, particularly the songs! But you Parisians take no interest in anything outside France! . . .

I should so like to know what you have been doing. My own work has become gayer, gentler, and more melodious in character, as I think you will see from the *Kinderszenen*. But they are mere bagatelles; I have attempted far more ambitious things.

How can you think I do not treasure your photograph? It is before me as I write. I should be glad to give you mine if you would tell me how to send it.

Dear Stamaty, I have an incomparable wife. There is no happiness equal to that. If you could

[1] See Letter 44.

only take a peep at us in our snug little artist home! Don't let it be long before you marry too. . . .

102.

To C. Kossmaly,[1] *at Detmold.*

LEIPZIG, *May* 9, 1841.

The paper still owes you a small sum, which I now enclose. I should like to send more than your due, but, as you know, I am now a householder, and circumstances have changed, though certainly not for the worse. Thank you for inquiring. I hope you will soon follow suit, and find a wife as good as mine. I have been very happy and busy since I last wrote.

I wish you knew my symphony.[2] The performance was a great joy to me—and to others. I really think it was received with more enthusiasm than any modern symphony since Beethoven. I am full of ideas for orchestral compositions, and have a number of things ready for performance next winter. The symphony will be published by the winter in any case, so you may perhaps hear it and give me your opinion. I was a little disappointed to find myself relegated to the second rank in your essay on song-writers. It is not that I claim a place in the first, but that I feel I deserve a place apart. I am anything but pleased to see myself

[1] Carl Kossmaly (1812-1893), a composer of songs and instrumental music, and a writer on musical subjects.

[2] In B flat, Op. 38. [Tr.]

classed with Reissiger, Curschmann, etc. My aims and my abilities are, I know, far higher, and I hope you will admit this without accusing me of vanity, which is far from me. I write with perfect frankness, and beg you will take my words in the right way, as addressed exclusively to one whose personality attracts me. . . .

103.

To C. Kossmaly.

LEIPZIG, *September* 1, 1842.

. . . I hope to achieve greater things in the future to justify your opinion of me. My past achievement gives me some satisfaction, but is trifling compared with the fair prospects which open up before me in occasional happy hours. What, in the way of music, do you think I pray for night and morning? German opera. There is an unworked mine! But neither must symphony be forgotten. . . .

104.

To H. C. Andersen,[1] *in Copenhagen.*

LEIPZIG, *October* 1, 1842.

What must you think of me for leaving your kind letter, which gave me such pleasure, so long unanswered! The fact is, I did not want to come to you quite empty-handed, although well aware I am now only returning what originally came

[1] Clara had made Andersen's acquaintance on her concert tour to Copenhagen in April, 1842.

to me from you. Please be indulgent to this musical setting of your poems. The music may seem strange to you at first, for so did your verses to me. As I grew more into the spirit of them my music took on a more exotic character, for which you are obviously responsible. Andersen's poems demand different treatment from 'Bloom, lovely violet,'[1] etc. . . .

I always insist on the minutest details when my wife talks about you, and I really believe I should recognize you if I met you casually. Did I not know you before from your poems—from the *Improvisatore*, *What the Moon Saw*, and especially *Only a Fiddler*, which is, indeed, the most delightful thing I know in modern Teutonic literature, excepting Immermann's ——.[2] Do I not possess a complete translation of your smaller poems, which doubtless still contain many pearls for the musician? May Heaven preserve you many years to your friends and admirers, with whom I beg to number myself.

105.

To L. Spohr.[3]

LEIPZIG, *November* 23, 1842.

We were much distressed to hear that you and your wife had called and missed us last summer.

[1] A children's song. [2] The title is illegible.

[3] Ludwig Spohr (1784-1859) had been director at Cassel since 1822. He was on friendly terms with Schumann, but did nothing to help him.

We looked for you everywhere that day, and only heard next morning of your hasty departure. My wife wanted you to hear her first trio, and I myself wished to show you one or two things. I hope this pleasure is only postponed until next summer, when you will delight your admirers by a long visit.

I had intended to send you my symphony, and ask your kind opinion of it, before I heard from our good friend Hauptmann of your wish to see it. You have only been able to judge me by my smaller efforts so far. I hope this more ambitious attempt will afford you some interest and pleasure. The symphony was written in the end of the winter of 1841. It was inspired, if I may say so, by the spirit of spring, which seems to possess us all anew every year, irrespective of age. The music is not intended to describe or paint anything definite, but I believe the season did much to shape the particular form it took. You will find it neither easy nor out-of-the-way difficult. I should like to point out one or two passages which have proved to be difficulties in every performance I have heard. . . .

I hope my music will reward you in some way for the pains you spend on it. I need hardly assure you of my gratitude. Your last symphony,[1] which I read over again yesterday with real profit to myself, convinces me, by its superiority over other works, how much I have still to learn. But

[1] '*Irdisches und Göttliches im Menschenleben.*'

a great master gains an added grace when, not content with creating beauty himself, he encourages youthful endeavour; and this letter may serve to express my gratitude to one whom I honour most among living artists.

106.

To C. Kossmaly.

LEIPZIG, *May* 5, 1843.

This will not be much of a letter. In front of my house some musicians from the fair are trying to deafen me, and indoors things are nearly as disturbing, for we have a christening to-morrow—our second girl.[1] But I must try to get this letter written to show you that I do appreciate your kind thought of me. Many thanks for your beautiful songs. I will keep back my opinion of them until it appears in the paper, as it very shortly will. How I wish you would publish more of your work, and come to Leipzig for good! Nothing positive is known about the changes at the theatre. A certain Dr. Schmidt is supposed to have taken it over. I know him slightly, and will find an opportunity of mentioning you.

The time since we met has been productive enough. Can you not arrange to have my three published quartets played over to you at Detmold? I particularly want you to hear them. A piano-

[1] There were eight children, four daughters and four sons. All were living when their father died, except one boy.

forte quintet is to appear shortly, also a pianoforte quartet and a few other things. I am now engaged on a great work, the greatest I have attempted so far. It is not an opera, but, as I rather think, a new departure for the concert-room.[1] I am putting all my energies into it, and hope to finish it in the course of the year.

It is with some timidity that I send you the accompanying parcel of my earlier compositions. You will realize their immaturity at a glance. They reflect for the most part the stormy scenes of my early life. The man and the musician in me have always struggled to manifest themselves simultaneously; indeed, this is still the case, although I have attained some degree of mastery over both. Your sympathetic heart will detect the joy and sadness that lie buried in this little pile of music.

I cannot, unfortunately, lay hands on a copy of what I consider my best pianoforte works—namely, *Kreisleriana*, six[2] *Phantasiestücke,* four books of *Novelletten*, and one of *Romanzen.* These are my last pianoforte compositions (written in 1838), but even from the earlier ones you will gain an insight into my character and aspirations. It is precisely in these early efforts that the germs of the future are discernible. I can only hope that, with all their faults, they may meet with your acceptance. They are but little known, and for obvious reasons: (1) they are too difficult in them-

[1] *Paradise and the Peri.* [2] Eight.

selves both as to form and meaning; (2) I am no virtuoso, and cannot play them in public; (3) I am an editor, and refrain of necessity from mentioning them in my paper; and (4) Fink, who edits another paper,[1] refrains from choice. But things are now taking a different turn. I am told that the public takes a greater interest in my works, the earlier ones included. The *Kinderszenen* and *Phantasiestücke*, which I am unable to send you, appeal, indeed, to a wide circle. Times have changed with me too. I used to be indifferent to the amount of notice I received, but a wife and children put a different complexion upon everything. It becomes imperative to think of the future, desirable to see the fruits of one's labour—not the artistic, but the prosaic fruits necessary to life; these fame helps to bring forth and multiply. So you must not set me down as vain for sending you these early pieces, which I have long outgrown, and for accepting with gratitude your kind offer to say a good word for them somewhere. I have always despised those artists who send off their trash, still damp from the printer's, post-haste to the various newspaper offices. But I need not waste words. You both know and understand me.

I think you will find some food for thought in my work, and have no difficulty in putting together a few columns about them. As most of them were published by Härtel's, they would probably be glad

[1] The *Allgemeine musikalische Zeitung*, published by Messrs. Breitkopf and Härtel. [Tr.]

to have something in their own paper on the subject. . . . I should prefer the article to take the form of an essay rather than the usual critical paragraph. . . .

So here you have my confessions. You will probably not need to be told that Bach and Jean-Paul influenced me more than anyone in former times. I hope I have now more independence. . . .

107.

To Johannes Verhulst,[1] *at the Hague.*

LEIPZIG, *June* 19, 1843.

Here is a letter at last, my dear Verhulst. I have had you in mind a hundred times and more, but, as you know, a musician prefers using musical notation to the alphabet, and I have written a quantity of music in the last three months. But more of that later.

Let me thank you first for your affectionate letter, which brought you before me as vividly as any portrait. Kindly thoughts, like yours, are always a comfort in one's struggles. You know my feelings towards you. Everything seems to augur a continuation of our present friendly relations. It was only to be expected that you would receive honour and distinction in your own country. I congratulate you on your decoration,[2] and wish,

[1] J. Verhulst (1816-1891), a distinguished composer of Mendelssohnian tendencies. He had been at Leipzig 1838-1842, and rendered excellent services later as a conductor in Holland.

[2] The Order of the Netherlands Lion. [Tr.]

above all, that your artist-heart may ever beat vigorously beneath your 'lion.' You should live to do great things, for you are young, sensible, and right-minded. I am looking forward to your new quartet. Please let us hear it at Inselstrasse[1] before long. Tell me, too, of your plans, and whether there is a chance of your coming to Leipzig soon. How often I miss you, at Poppe's[2] and in my walks. No one else is so quick at entering into my ideas and opinions. I am often silent by the hour together of an evening, now that you are not here. Kirchner[3] alone has a real soul for music, but I cannot talk to him as freely as to an older man. It would rather harm than help him.

You have already heard that we played a good deal in the winter, some of my new things amongst others. Parts of my quintet and quartet will appeal to you, for they have life in them. I have not yet heard the trio,[4] which is different, more subdued in character. We are hoping to try it one of these days, when Rietz[5] returns. He is our 'cellist, a splendid fellow and musician. The *Variations* for two pianofortes, etc., I have only heard

[1] Schumann lived at No. 5, Inselstrasse, after his marriage.

[2] A restaurant where Schumann regularly spent an hour or two in the evening. [Tr.]

[3] Theodor Kirchner (1823-1903) closely resembled Schumann in his nature, as his unduly neglected compositions show.

[4] In A minor.

[5] Julius Rietz (1812-1877), a well-known composer and a conductor of note.

once. They did not go particularly well. They need considerable study. I must have been in a melancholy mood when I wrote them, for they leave a mournful impression.

My chief item of news is that I finished *Paradise and the Peri* last Friday. It is my longest work and, I think, my best. As I wrote *finis* on the last sheet of the score, I felt so thankful that my strength had been equal to the strain. A work of these dimensions is no light undertaking. I realize better now what it means to write a succession of them, such as, for instance, the eight operas which Mozart produced within so short a time. Have I told you the story of the Peri? If not, do make an effort to get it. You will find it in Moore's *Lalla Rookh.* It is simply made for music. The whole conception is so poetic and ideal that I was quite carried away by it. The music is just long enough for an evening performance. I expect and really hope to give it at a concert of my own next winter, and possibly to conduct it myself. *You must certainly come.* I hope my labours may again be rewarded by your kind, approving smile.

I could find much more to say to you, but it is impossible to put it all in one letter. We are all well. Clara presented me with another daughter on the 25th of April. She is doing very well, and wishes to be remembered to you. Our eldest little girl grows more delightful every day, and is developing rapidly in mind and body. There has been a reconciliation between Clara and her father.

I am glad of it for her sake, but the man must be quite devoid of decent feeling to attempt to renew his acquaintance with myself, as he actually is doing. But at last the clouds are lifting, and I am very glad on Clara's account.[1]

Sometimes I see much of Mendelssohn, at others little. We are both so much engaged that we often do not exchange a word for weeks together. The Conservatorium keeps us all occupied. It should, I think, prove an important factor in the training of Germany's future musicians. Kirchner, who has entered himself as a student, has undoubtedly more talent for composition than any of them. . . .

108.

To Dr. E. Krüger.[2]

Undated [LEIPZIG, *October*, 1844].

The thought of my remissness towards you has often distressed me. You may not perhaps know

[1] A reconciliation did eventually take place between Schumann and his father-in-law, impossible as it seemed at the time when Wieck was convicted for insulting him (1841), and showed such meanness on the question of Clara's money. The change came suddenly in January, 1843. Wieck saw that he was only injuring his own position by his attitude at a time when Schumann's fame was steadily increasing. Clara was only too delighted to clasp the outstretched hand, and Schumann's satisfaction over this is a proof of his delicacy. In December, 1843, Wieck made overtures to his son-in-law, which were accepted. Cordial relations, indeed, were never resumed. There was even renewed coolness, although amicable public relations were preserved.

[2] Dr. Eduard Krüger (1805-1885), co-rector at Emden, was more successful as a critic than as a composer. Schumann was

that I have had a serious nervous illness for the past three months, and was, in consequence, forbidden every exertion, mental or physical, by my doctor. I am now a little better, and can see some brightness in life, some return of hope and confidence. I think I did too much music. My music to Goethe's *Faust* occupied me very much latterly, and in the end mind and body both gave way. . . . During this time I have not been able to hear a note of music, for it was like a knife to my nerves. . . .

(*Written from Dresden, five weeks later.*)

I am still suffering, and have moments of despondency. Work is forbidden me ; I may only rest and take walks—and even these I often find exhausting. Oh for the return of spring to bring me back my strength ! . . . We have come to Dresden for the winter. The doctor advised it, and we complied the more readily as Mendelssohn's departure from Leipzig had completely unsettled us in our musical life. All the same, Leipzig is still the most important musical centre, and I should advise every talented student to go there, for he will hear, not only much music, but much good music. . . .

My *Faust* music still makes great demands on my time. What should you say to using the whole material for an oratorio ? Is it not a bold

---

so displeased by Krüger's criticism of his *Genoveva* that their intercourse was discontinued.

and happy idea? But I must content myself with thinking of it for the present.

109.

To Mendelssohn at Leipzig.

Undated [Written about the end of September, 1845].

It was my turn to write—to thank you for your kind visit, and for much that you said. But writing of any sort still tires me very much, therefore forgive me. I am already rather better. Hofrat Carus has advised early morning walks, which have done me a lot of good. Yet I am not altogether cured, and I have touches of pain every day in a hundred different places. A mysterious illness, which seems to vanish when the doctor prepares to attack it! But better times will come again, and I am happy enough when I look on my wife and children.

My wife confidently expects to be in Leipzig in time to play at the first concert. We have decided on Henselt's concerto, as we hope to give a concert on our own account later on, when she will play mine. My wife also commissions me to say that she would like to play only that one number. The concerto is as difficult as two ordinary concertos, and very exhausting; in short, she would rather not undertake to play anything besides. Will you be so kind as to communicate this to the directors? A special rehearsal is not necessary; therefore we shall not be in Leipzig before Friday. Just a line, please, to tell us when the general rehearsal is. For days my head has been a whirl of drums and trumpets (trombe in C). I don't know what will come of it.[1]

110.

To Mendelssohn at Leipzig.

DRESDEN, *October* 22, 1845. *Wednesday morning.*

DEAR MENDELSSOHN,

You must now be well in the middle of my symphony. Do you still remember the first rehearsal of it in the year 1841—and the 'stopped' trumpets and horns at the beginning? It sounded as if the orchestra had a cold in its head; I can't help laughing when I think of it. And now let me thank you for again thinking about my piece and again taking trouble over it. It is with the greatest pleasure that I think of that first evening's performance. How beautifully it went, better than I have ever heard it since! I might perhaps repeat the experience to-morrow, but I dare not come. I am sorry to say that I have not yet regained my full strength; every divergence from my simple régime upsets me, and induces morbid irritability. That is why I reluctantly stayed away when my wife was with you. I must avoid every form of gaiety. There is nothing for it but to go on hoping, and that I am determined to do.

[1] What came of it was Schumann's second symphony in C, Op. 61.

Clara told me with genuine pleasure how good and kind you had been. You know she is an old admirer of yours, and is happy at your least sign of approval. For her untiring zeal and energy in her art she really deserves every one's love and encouragement; then, as a woman, she is indeed a gift from Heaven. So, you see, she came back from Leipzig quite delighted, frankly admitting that you were the chief cause of her delight. Lately we have been absorbed in your organ sonatas, unfortunately with the piano as substitute; but we should have discovered that they were yours without the name on the cover. They are stamped on every page with that striving after perfection which makes me look to you as my model. Then the poetry and originality of the form! Each sonata is rounded off to a complete picture. Bach's music gives me the impression of himself seated at the organ, but yours brings me a vision of a Cecilia fingering the keys. How charming that that should be your wife's name, too! The fifth and sixth struck me as being the most important. One thing is certain, dear Mendelssohn, no one but you writes harmonies so pure, harmonies ever-increasing in purity and spiritual beauty. Have I been praising you again? May I? What, indeed, does the world in general (many so-called musicians included) understand of pure harmony? There is Wagner, who has just finished another opera.[1] He is certainly a clever fellow, full of crazy ideas and

[1] *Tannhäuser.*

audacious to a degree. Society still raves over *Rienzi.* Yet he cannot write or think out four consecutive bars of beautiful, hardly of good music. All these young musicians are weak in harmony, in the art of four-part writing. How can enduring work be produced in that way? And now we can see the whole score in print, fifths, octaves and all. It is too late now to alter and scratch out, however much he may wish it. The music is no fraction better than *Rienzi*, but duller and more unnatural, if anything. If one says anything of the sort it is always put down to envy, and that is why I only say it to you, knowing you have long been of the same opinion. . . .

(*From a letter written on November* 12.)

. . . I may have a chance of talking to you about *Tannhäuser* soon. *I must take back one or two things* I said after reading the score. It makes quite a different effect on the stage. Much of it impressed me deeply (*cf.* Letter 126).

111.

To Ludwig Meinardus,[1] *at the Jever Gymnasium.*

DRESDEN, *September* 3, 1846.

MY DEAR YOUNG FRIEND,

You must think me unkind to have let you wait so long for an answer. But at the seaside[2] all

[1] Ludwig Meinardus (1827-1896) became a well-known composer and writer on music.

[2] Nordeney.

exertion is forbidden; indeed, it forbids itself. I have been so ill for a long time now that I can hardly write more than one letter at a time. Therefore, forgive the long delay in answering your kind note, which was particularly welcome in the monotony of seaside life. I have been thinking about you a great deal, have read much of your letter many times, and was pleased with the youthful spirit, as well as with the many clear, practical views expressed in it. All things considered, I should like to call your attention to one or two points before you come to a decision. I was once in a similar position to yours, had to do with an anxious mother, and to fight local prejudices in a small town. At the critical moment fairly favourable outside circumstances came to my help; things fell out as they were bound to do. I became a musician, and my mother was happy in my happiness. But for those favourable outside circumstances who knows what would have become of me, or whether I should have defeated the fate to which talent without means so often falls a prey. I cannot say how sorry I am to have to draw your attention precisely to that passage in your letter where you write to me so frankly and confidingly about your circumstances. You yourself thought the matter of sufficient importance to tell me, and you were right. Will your courage carry you through the long time which must elapse before there is even a possibility of an assured position for you? Will not the thousand deprivations and humiliations rob you of your youthful strength and creative faculty? In this respect, it seems to me, you have far overestimated your own powers. You would have much to catch up, many things to learn that young musicians of your age have left far behind them long ago. You would certainly have to face a stern discipline. That you might eventually become a good, possibly a great, composer, I can believe from the talent shown in your compositions. But no voice reaches us from the future, for which we have no guarantee.

My advice, then, is: keep your love for art; practise yourself in composition as much as possible; hold fast to the great models and masters, especially to Bach, Mozart, and Beethoven, not forgetting the present in which you live. But before you decide to follow the career on which your heart is set, subject yourself to the severest self-examination, and if you find you are not strong enough to defy its troubles and dangers, then seek a firm foundation, which you can always adorn with the pictures of your fancy and with those of your most loved artists. That you should keep a kindly recollection of me would please me as your whole letter has done. Let me hear of your work from time to time. Write to me presently about your immediate decisions, and tell me whether you agree with anything in my letter.

112.

To Friedrich Hebbel[1] *in Vienna.*

DRESDEN, *May* 14, 1847.

MY VERY DEAR SIR,

Excuse the freedom taken by one who is possibly quite unknown to you in preferring a request, the fulfilment of which lies entirely with you, and would give great pleasure to your petitioner.

In reading your poem *Genoveva* (I am a musician), I was struck by the magnificent material which it offers for music. The oftener I read your unrivalled tragedy — I will not attempt further praise—the more vividly did I see it in its musical form. Finally, I consulted a man living here who is something of a poet.[2] He was immediately impressed by the extraordinary beauty of the poem, and readily consented to try to arrange it as an operatic libretto.

Two acts lie before me, and I shall shortly receive the other two. But although the adapter has done his best, it is not what I want. It is weak throughout. I very much dislike the ordinary libretto style, and neither can nor will write music for tirades of that sort.

I was almost in despair, when it occurred to me that the direct way might be the best, and I decided to address myself to the original poet, and to ask

[1] Friedrich Hebbel, dramatic poet (1813-1863). [Tr.]

[2] Robert Reinick.

for his assistance. But do not, dear Sir, misunderstand me. I do not suggest that you should adapt for operatic purposes a work so profound in its conception, so masterly in its form, but that you should look over the adaptation, tell me what you think, and give it an inspiring touch here and there. This is what I have to ask.

Is it in vain? It is your own child that asks for protection. And if it should meet your eye in its musical form, I should like you to say that you loved it in that form also.[1] In the meantime I have been reading *Judith*—the world is not in such bad case after all! While poets of the *Genoveva* and *Judith* calibre still live, we are a long way from the fall of poetry. An answer, if you are so good as to send one, will reach me here. If it brings consent, I shall thank you as I can; if a refusal, count me at least among your most genuine admirers, and give me the opportunity of proving it. . . .

One thing more: we must all live. If you give your attention to this, you will be neglecting other work. Naturally, we should have to discuss this point.

[1] Hebbel did not care to see his work cut down for a libretto, and would have nothing to do with altering it. Schumann finally arranged his own text. [Tr.]

113.

To F. Brendel.[1]

DRESDEN, *August* 8, 1847.

DEAR FRIEND,

Accept my hearty congratulations on the inauguration of your scheme, which must have entailed much care and trouble in the preliminary stages. I may be able to drop in for an hour or so myself, but of that later.

I have been defining my propositions more accurately this morning, and find that my chief difficulty lies in choosing a form of expression. If I had time to work them out in separate essays, this would certainly be best. But it would take time, a great deal of it, especially as I am past the alphabet stage. I think the most profitable way will be for me to give you a brief outline of my ideas, from which you can select anything you think suited for public discussion, mentioning my name or not, as you please.

First, then, I think it desirable that a section should detach itself from the Convention to consider *the protection of classical music against modern adaptations.*

The duties of the section would be to obtain

[1] Franz Brendel (1811-1868) was from 1845 manager of the *Neue Zeitschrift für Musik.* The letter refers to the foundation of a Universal German Society of Musicians. The first meeting of the founders was on August 13 and 14, 1847. Schumann took no part in it, but Brendel read out the letter and brought forward his proposals for discussion.

information of all such publications—that is, of all new editions of old compositions of importance; to see how far the original was left untouched, or whether unwarranted alterations had been made; and finally to report on the result of their labours at the next (as I hope) annual meeting of the Convention.

I should then like to propose that another section be formed for *the research and restoration of corrupted passages in classical works,* in the sense in which I dealt with it in my essay: *On Some Presumably Corrupted Passages in the Works of Bach, Mozart, and Beethoven* (*Neue Zeitschrift für Musik,* vol. xv., p. 149).[1]

This section would, like the first, be required to search out and collect the necessary material to lay before the next meeting. The result would be some interesting and thoroughly practical debates.

The section given up to minute inquiry would render a very great service, for instance, by looking into Mozart's *Requiem,* about which the grossest misconceptions are still current, for the existing version is not merely corrupt, but, except for certain numbers, spurious.

I should next like to raise the question of *the use of French for titles,* also *the misuse of Italian for marks of expression,* by Germans in their own compositions. I should be glad if you would move *the*

[1] Schumann's *Gesammelte Schriften* (ii., p. 344).

abolition of French titles, and *the rejection of such Italian expressions as may be rendered as well, if not better, in German.*

Finally, the Convention should consider by what means their future meetings, which will become, it is to be hoped, an annual institution, may be made to *benefit and encourage youthful composers especially.* This end might be assured by a public invitation, issued by a section told off for the purpose, to composers to send in manuscripts of any important works (such as oratorios, masses, symphonies, string quartets), the best of which would be selected for performance at the next general Convention; or, again, by announcing a prize competition, or in some other way.

These, my dear Brendel, are my suggestions, which I leave you to bring forward, either as your own or in any way you please. I feel how much easier it would be to say all this in a few rapid, forcible words than to write it.

And now I want to ask you, if you are not too busy, to send me a line with the proposed programme for both days, the 13th and 14th; I should like to know how the time is to be divided, and also if anything will be done on Sunday. I may perhaps come for Saturday or Sunday.

I was surprised to hear that you had chosen a president, as I think this should have been done in full council. But I may be mistaken.

114.

To Director D. G. Otten,[1] *at Hamburg.*

DRESDEN, *April 2*, 1849.

DEAR SIR,

You must be thinking me a strange person to have left your kind letter[2] so long unanswered. But, indeed, I have been thinking of both you and your letter, for which I now thank you, contenting myself with the old excuse that we musicians are readier at musical notation than the written word.

I wrote my symphony in December, 1845, and I sometimes fear my semi-invalid state can be divined from the music. I began to feel more myself when I wrote the last movement, and was certainly much better when I finished the whole work. All the same, it reminds me of dark days. Your interest in a work so stamped with melancholy proves your real sympathy. Everything you say proves your thorough acquaintance with the music, and I was greatly delighted to find that my mournful bassoon in the Adagio was not lost upon you, for I confess I wrote that part for it with peculiar pleasure.

I have long known your zeal in the cause of good music, particularly as expressed in your concert society. The news of good work is carried, independently of newspapers, you see, by kind,

[1] G. D. Otten (*b.* 1806) founded and conducted the Hamburg Musical Society.

[2] About the C major symphony.

invisible spirits. For about a year now I have been running a similar concert society, which affords me the delight of hearing the works of Palestrina, Bach, and various neglected compositions.

Do you know Bach's Passion-Music according to St. John, the so-called little one? But of course you do. I wonder if you agree with me that it is much bolder, more powerful and poetical, than the St. Matthew version? The *St. Matthew* seems to me the earlier of the two by five or six years, rather drawn out in places and of excessive length; in the *St. John* what terseness, what inspiration, especially in the choruses, and what consummate art![1] If only such questions could be cleared up! But they are never discussed, except very occasionally by musical papers; and even then these matters are rarely threshed out, simply because the writer lacks real knowledge and real conviction. So things are, and will remain. After all, something must be left for the few scattered, genuine music-lovers who care about Bach, Palestrina, Beethoven's later quartets, etc. 'Forward' is, then, my greeting to you. Let us be united in the untiring effort to give honour where honour is due, and virtue will bring its own reward.

[1] The St. John version is, nevertheless, always considered inferior to the St. Matthew, although it has every claim to rank beside it as a masterpiece. Schumann was wrong in thinking the St. Matthew the earlier, as it was written six years later than the St. John (1723)

115.

To Franz Liszt at Weimar.

BAD KREISCHA, *near* DRESDEN, *May* 31, 1849.

DEAR FRIEND,

Herr Reinecke's[1] stay in Dresden was so brief that I could give him no definite answer to your question referring to the scene from *Faust*. Indeed, we had only met once, when the Revolution scattered us in all directions. But the piece is too short, considering the expense it would entail to produce; I always meant to lengthen it by adding other scenes from the drama, and still hope to do so. I would rather not produce it in its present form.

But would not the thing be too Leipzigian[2] for you in any case? Or is it possible that you do consider Leipzig a miniature Paris, in which we can turn out good work? Seriously, I hardly expected such a sweeping judgment on my career from you, who knew so much of my work. If you will examine my compositions, you cannot fail to

[1] Karl Reinecke (*b.* 1824), the composer, for many years conductor of the Gewandhaus concerts at Leipzig.

[2] This refers to a slight dispute of Schumann's with Liszt on the evening of June 9, 1848, when Liszt, who had already annoyed Schumann by his unpunctuality, had made some disparaging remarks about Leipzig and Mendelssohn, which called forth a passionate demonstration from the usually silent Schumann. Liszt, who felt that he had been to blame in the first instance, knew how to smooth over the difficulties of this occurrence, and never bore any grudge against Schumann, whom he genuinely respected.

find a considerable amount of variety in them, for I have always sought to make each one fresh, not only in form, but in idea. And really, you know, our little group at Leipzig was not so bad, including as it did Mendelssohn, Hiller, and Bennett; at least, we did not compare unfavourably with the Parisians, Viennese, and Berliners. If a common trait distinguishes our compositions as a group, call it philistinism or what you will, all artistic epochs show a similar phenomenon. Take Bach, Händel and Gluck, or Mozart, Haydn and Beethoven, respectively, and you will find a hundred instances of perplexing similarity in their work. I must except Beethoven's last compositions, although they again revert to Bach. No one is entirely original. But I have said enough. Your remark was an unjustifiable affront; but we will forget that evening. Words do not kill; the main thing is to keep pressing forwards.

Reinecke tells me you are staying some time at W[eimar]. Shall you come over to Leipzig when my opera is performed, probably at the end of August? I will let you know the exact date later, if you like. I suppose a performance at W[eimar] could be arranged for the winter with your help. I should be very glad if it could be done.

Since the Revolution banished us we have lived peacefully here, and my appetite for work increases, if anything, in spite of my being preoccupied by public events. All last year I worked hard, and lately without interruptions; so there will be a good deal published shortly, great and small. I have practically finished one rather big thing—the music to Byron's *Manfred.* It is arranged for dramatic performance with an overture, entr'actes, and other occasional music for which the text gives ample scope. . . .

116.

To F. Brendel.

DRESDEN, *September* 18, 1849.

I am delighted with all your notices of *Faust.* I knew before the performance what the effect on the public would be,[1] and was, therefore, not surprised; but I knew also that my music would appeal to individual hearers. I have never been satisfied with the final chorus, as you heard it, and have written a second and far more satisfactory version. But as the parts of the new one were not written out, I chose the other. The second version will certainly be sung at the next performance at Leipzig, when I hope to include some of the first part of *Faust* in the programme.

You are mistaken about Rietz,[2] who is perfectly upright in his profession, as I can prove abundantly. He has shown the greatest sympathy with my efforts, as, indeed, he could not fail to do, being what he is. An artist who refuses to recognize honest work among his contemporaries must be

[1] *Faust* met with very slight success.

[2] Julius Rietz (1812-1877), a well-known composer and conductor.

numbered with the lost, from which company I hope you will now remove Rietz.

In any case, I fail to see the non-recognition from which I am supposed to suffer. Appreciation often falls to my lot in full measure; your journal provides many instances. Another practical but very convincing proof is offered by the publishers, who show a certain desire for my compositions, and pay high prices for them. I don't like speaking of these things, but I may tell you in confidence that my *Jugendalbum*, for instance, has a sale equalled by few, if any, among recent compositions. This I have from the publisher himself; and many of my books of songs enjoy the same popularity. And which composer ever found an immediate circulation for *all* his works? Take Mendelssohn's *Variations* in D minor—an admirable work—is its circulation a quarter of that which the *Songs without Words* enjoy, for instance? And then, where is the composer whose fame is universal? Where is the work—were it even of Divine origin—universally acknowledged as sacred? I have spared no pains, it is true, but have plodded on for twenty years, careless of praise or blame, intent on proving my claim to be called a true servant of art. But do you think there is no satisfaction in reading such mention as you and others have often made of my work? Let me assure you again of my entire satisfaction with the recognition I have received up to now in ever-increasing measure. . . .

117.

To F. Hiller.

DRESDEN, *November* 19, 1849.

Many thanks for your letter. Your suggestion[1] is very attractive, but I have some doubts. In both respects, my thoughts must be much the same as yours before you decided to accept the post. I have a clear recollection of Mendelssohn's verdict on the Düsseldorf musicians, which was bad enough. Rietz, too, when you went from here to D[üsseldorf], wondered 'how you came to take the post.' I said nothing to you then for fear of depressing you. I beg you, dear Hiller, to tell me the unvarnished truth about it. It is rare to find good manners among members of any orchestra, and I know how to deal with merely vulgar, though not with rude or malicious, players.

I must now ask you to inform me on one or two points. It will be best to take them in order:

1. Is it a municipal appointment? Who are the chief members of the committee? 2. The salary is 750 talers—not gulden? 3. How large are chorus and orchestra? 4. Is living as dear there as here, for instance? What do you pay for your lodgings? 5. Are furnished lodgings to be had? 6. Would it be possible to obtain slight compensation for the removal and the expensive

[1] To take over, as Hiller's successor, the post of musical director at Düsseldorf.

journey? 7. Could the contract be so worded as to leave me free to resign, and accept any other post that might offer? 8. Are the practices of the society continued through the summer? 9. Would there be time for short excursions of a week or a fortnight in the winter? 10. Could my wife find any scope for work? You know how impossible it is to her to be idle.

One more important question. I could not leave here before next Easter, as my opera is to be put into rehearsal at Leipzig in February for certain, and probably at Frankfurt soon after, when my presence will be necessary. If you will clear up these points for me, we can then discuss matters further. It will go hard with us to leave Saxony, yet it is salutary to leave the accustomed groove and seek a new sphere. We are very much occupied at present. Clara is giving a series of successful recitals with Schubert.[1] There is a performance of the *Peri* in prospect, besides which I am kept busy by a number of things I have on hand. More of that in my next letter. Let me thank you once more for your kind thought of me in this matter. May my good genius lead me to the right decision. My wife sends kindest remembrances to your wife as to yourself.

[1] The brothers Franz (1808-1878) and Friedrich (*d.* 1853) Schubert were highly esteemed members of the Court orchestra in Dresden, the former being leader of the orchestra and the latter a violoncellist.

118.

To F. Hiller.

DRESDEN, *December* 3, 1849.

DEAR HILLER,

I have been suffering all this time from a headache, which kept me from working or thinking; hence my delay in answering. I am more and more drawn to Düsseldorf after all you have said in your letter. Could you let me know when you think the committee would want my final decision as to accepting the post? I should prefer to leave it until Easter, if I might. I will tell you my reason later. One thing more: I was looking up Düsseldorf in an old geography the other day, and found, amongst the attractions, three convents and an asylum. I might put up with the convents, but it made me uncomfortable to read of the other. I must explain to you: some years ago, when, as you remember, we lived at Maxen, I discovered that I had from my window a full view of Sonnenstein.[1] This outlook came latterly to affect me seriously—indeed, it spoilt my whole stay, and I now fear that it might be the same at Düsseldorf. But, of course, the geography may be at fault, and the institution nothing more than a hospital, such as there is in every town.

I have to avoid very carefully any depressing associations of the kind. We musicians, as you are

[1] An asylum.

well aware, are often exalted to the heights; but the sight of the naked misery of real life wounds the more deeply. At least, this is the case with me, thanks to my vivid imagination. I remember reading something of the kind in Goethe too—*sans comparaison!*

119.

To R. Pohl.[1]

DÜSSELDORF, *February* 14, 1851.

DEAR SIR,

I am sending you an outline[2] which agrees on the whole with your own. My chief endeavour was to arrive at clearness as to the *musical* form. We have such a mass of material that it will need careful sifting. We must reject all that is not essential to the development, including, I think, the supernatural apparitions. The ghost of Huss seems to me the only one suitable to retain.

I have so many things to tell you, but must confine myself to the most urgent to-day.

The oratorio must be equally suitable for church or concert performances, and must not exceed two and a half hours in length, intervals included. The narrative, reasoning style should be avoided as much as possible, to keep it dramatic in form. It should be accurate historically, especially in the reproduction of Luther's well-known pithy remarks.

[1] R. Pohl (1826-1896), known under the pseudonym of 'Hoplit' as a writer on music of New German tendencies. He lived at Weimar.

[2] Of an oratorio on Luther.

Please give me all the opportunities you can of introducing chorus. You probably know Händel's *Israel in Egypt*, which is to me a model of choral composition. I should like the chorus in *Luther* to fill as important a part. I should like some double choruses, too, especially at the close of each section. A soprano part is absolutely necessary. I imagine Katharina could be introduced very effectively. Neither must you omit the wedding (in the third part). The chorale *Ein' feste Burg* must be saved for the grand finale, and sung as a chorus.

I suppose we must give up Hutten, Sickingen, Hans Sachs, Lukas Kranach, and the Princes Palatine, Friedrich and Johann Philipp of Hesse, which is a pity. But if we increase the number of solo parts, we shall have great difficulty in finding singers for them at every performance. It seems to me hardly possible to introduce parts of the German Mass into the different sections, but the chorale will be a splendid substitute. Luther's relation to music and his love for it, which may be traced in a hundred of his charming sayings, should be expressed in some way. An alto or second soprano part is still to be considered. I quite agree about the metrical treatment of the text and the popular old German tone of the whole. The music should, I think, have the same character, and aim at effect rather by its conciseness, strength, and clearness than by its elaboration.

We are on the verge of an undertaking, my dear

sir, which is well worth a special effort, and needs both courage and humility. Let me thank you for your ready co-operation. We shall need all our energy and perseverance to accomplish such a task.

120.

To Moritz Horn,[1] *at Chemnitz.*

DÜSSELDORF, *April* 21, 1851.

I have been so pressed by various business matters that I could not acknowledge your packet before to-day. The poem[2] is undoubtedly suitable for setting to music, and has already sent a crowd of melodies surging through my brain; but it would have to be shortened in many places, and more dramatic as a whole. I say this purely with a view to a musical setting, and am far from criticizing the poem as such.

I have ventured to note on the enclosed paper a few suggestions for alterations. Up to the words

'und bittet freundlich hier
Um Obdach'

everything is favourable to musical treatment. From that point onwards there would have to be more variety, more dramatic development.

If you could bring yourself to make certain alterations, purely in consideration of the music, I should be very glad to use the poem. It is so fresh in my memory that the sooner you can take

[1] Moritz Horn (1814-1874) was an actuary at Chemnitz.

[2] *The Pilgrimage of the Rose.*

the matter in hand the better pleased I shall be. If you publish your poem you could keep its present form, while the musical version might bear the inscription, '*After* a poem by,' etc. . . .

121.

To R. Pohl.

DÜSSELDORF, *May* 13, 1851.

The past weeks have been so taken up by rehearsals, performances, and other business, that I have hardly been able to give a thought to anything else. I owe you so many thanks for the instalment you sent me. I am more than ever convinced, on seeing the serious character of your work, that our united energies should produce something good. But I am not sure that we can build upon this beginning.[1] The music to the introduction alone would take up a whole evening, and is therefore too long, much as the ideas contained in it appeal to me. The plan of dividing the oratorio into two parts, to be performed on different days, is one to which I cannot reconcile myself, nor do I think it advisable.

What is to be done? We must, I think, reduce the material to the simplest outline, or select a few only of the important events in Luther's life. The supernatural element should be sparingly introduced, for it does not seem to me to suit the

[1] The first part of a trilogy on Luther which Pohl had planned out. Unfortunately, Schumann's work was never written.

character of the Reformer at all. We know him to have been upright, manly, and self-reliant.

It is so difficult to explain this sort of thing by letter. Everything could be arranged in half the time if we lived together for a while, as I could wish.

I should be grieved indeed to hear that the difficulties had induced you to give up the work altogether. I was looking forward to making some progress with it this summer. Please let me know soon what you really think, and whether the difficulties in the way of carrying out the splendid idea that possesses us are to be surmounted.

122.

To J. N., at T.

DÜSSELDORF, *September* 22, 1851.

DEAR SIR,

In thanking you for your promptness in sending me a copy of your work, I must, on the other hand, protest against another part of your letter,[1] which seems, considering my position and your own, to display an arrogant presumption. By what right do you, who have as yet given to the world no proof of artistic or critical ability, take upon yourself to bestow, upon one who can

[1] This letter is only included to show how decided Schumann could be. J. N. had sent Schumann an operatic libretto, *Beatrice*, and used the opportunity to advise him to forswear his romantic tendencies.

at least point to some small achievements, such reprimands as are given to a beginner? Did you not take this into account? You tell me nothing that I did not know thirty years ago—nothing that I did not instil into my pupils at the Leipzig Conservatorium nearly ten years ago.

My compositions—the larger works especially—might, I imagine, convince you of my acquaintance with the great masters. It is *to them* I go, and have always gone, for advice: to Gluck the simple, to Händel the complicated, and to Bach the most complicated of all. Let me commend you to the study of Bach; my most complicated works will thereafter seem simple enough. Have you also failed to glean from my music that I do not write with the sole intent to please children and amateurs? As if all mental pictures must be shaped to fit one or two forms; as if each idea did not come into existence with its form ready-made; as if each work of art had not necessarily its own meaning, and consequently its own form! Jean Paul is worth a hundred of your Herr O. von Redwitz to me; and I prefer Shakespeare to Jean Paul.

This is my reply to your letter, of which tone and contents were alike insulting. I should not dream of undertaking a subject which lends itself less than any to so-called 'simplicity' of treatment, even were it better suited to the spirit of the age than I deem it. It would be as well to prepare yourself for a few thunder-claps in any music written to *Beatrice,* however imbecile the composer!

123.

To Franz Liszt.

DÜSSELDORF, *December* 25, 1851.

I am returning *Manfred* herewith. I have examined text and music again, with the assistance of Hildebrandt and Wolfgang Müller, and I think it may now be risked on the stage.[1]

I am now convinced that all the apparitions must come on as real people. I intend writing to Herr Genast[2] later about certain of the stage arrangements. As to the music, dear friend, I hope you will like the overture. I really consider it one of the finest of my brain-children, and wish you may agree with me. In the melodramatic portions, where the music accompanies the voice, half the strings would be sufficient, I imagine. These matters can be decided at rehearsal. The main thing is still, of course, the impersonation of Manfred, for whom the music is but a setting. I should be very grateful if you could assist in bringing home to the Weimar actors the importance of this fine part.

We are all quite well at home. My wife and the children are all recovered. Please convey our thanks to the Princess for her kind letter of sympathy. My wife will enclose a note in this. One

[1] Liszt carried out this attempt successfully on June 13, 1852.

[2] Manager of the Weimar theatre.

more greeting to you before the old year dies, and let me count on your lasting affection.

124.

To F. Hebbel.

DÜSSELDORF, *March* 14, 1853.

How I should like to send, along with your *Nachtlied*,[1] an army of musicians and singers to serenade you to sleep on the evening of the 18th[2] with your own verses! But I must be content to offer it you as it is. Let me thank you for your most kind letter, of which I value every word, and for the copy of *Michel Angelo*.[3] What a delightful description it gives of the sensitive side of an artist's nature!

I must hope for an early opportunity both of thanking you in person for your poems, which have given, and continue to give me keen emotional enjoyment, and of absorbing myself in them with a view to composition.

My wife wishes to be remembered to you in return for your kind inquiries. Please present our united kind regards to Frau Hebbel. You and I are, I consider, highly favoured in having two great

[1] Op. 108, for chorus and orchestra; dedicated to Hebbel. [Tr.]

[2] His birthday.

[3] Hebbel had presented Schumann with the MS. of his drama, *Michel Angelo*. The printed edition (1855) is dedicated to Schumann.

artists[1] for our helpmates, who not only appreciate our efforts better than anyone, but are also able to interpret them. I will take leave of you to-day with this pleasant reflection, and with the hope of your continued regard.

125.

To Director H. Krigar[2] *in Berlin.*

DÜSSELDORF, *March* 16, 1853.

DEAR SIR,

Accept my thanks for the music.[3] I shall, no doubt, need to double and treble them after closer perusal. It gives me the greatest pleasure to meet with a composition of such lofty character as the *De profundis.* I know nothing to compare with it in modern church music. It seems to me a masterpiece in every respect. Apart from the skilful phrasing displayed in every part of the psalm, which is such as we only find in Bach, from the masterly and original contrapuntal treatment, and all the qualities that proclaim the master-hand, it impresses by its deeply religious character. It bears the convincing stamp of personal faith, and I feel sure its effect will be deep and lasting. Had I

[1] Hebbel's wife, Christiana Enghaus, had been an actress at the Hofburg theatre.

[2] Hermann Krigar (1819-1880), pupil of the Leipzig Conservatorium and a music-teacher in Berlin.

[3] The composition was a *De profundis,* set for quadruple chorus by F. E. Wilsing (*b.* 1809). It was awarded a gold medal by Friedrich Wilhelm IV., and was performed at Leipzig through Schumann's influence.

seen it sooner, I might perhaps have secured its performance at the next Rhine Festival; but the programme is now arranged, and cannot be altered. The work should obtain a hearing in your own capital, where all facilities are available. It would be a scandal if this prophet, too, should have to seek his honour from strangers. Can you not set the matter in motion?

Thank you once more for sending me the psalm, which I might otherwise have missed seeing for some time. The composer should, judging by the high standard of the music, be too strong-minded to care about outside opinion; but if you think he would be gratified by the assurance of a brother-composer's entire sympathy, please give him mine. . . .

126.

To C. v. Bruyck.[1]

DÜSSELDORF, *May* 8, 1853.

MY VERY DEAR SIR,

I delayed answering your kind letter until I received *Schön Hedwig*,[2] which has just arrived. I have much pleasure in enclosing it; will you please give the second copy to Dr. Hebbel, with my kind regards? The form of the composition is, I think, entirely novel. We so often have to

[1] Carl Debrois von Bruyck (1828-1902), a composer and writer on music in Vienna. He also wrote on Schumann.

[2] Op. 106, a ballad by Hebbel, set by Schumann as a declamation with pianoforte accompaniment. [Tr.]

thank the poets for inspiration to seek out new paths in art.

Many thanks, too, for your last sympathetic letter. I should like you to hear my larger orchestral works; for, although I may say I bestow the same care on my smaller works, the handling of a mass of material demands quite a different concentration of energy.

I was much interested in what you said about Wagner. He is, to put it concisely, not a good musician. He has no sense of form or euphony. You must not, however, judge by pianoforte arrangements of his scores. Many parts of his operas could not fail to stir you deeply if you heard them on the stage. If his genius does not send out rays of pure sunlight, it exercises at times a mysterious charm over the senses. Yet, I repeat, the music, considered apart from the setting, is inferior—often quite amateurish, meaningless and repugnant; and it is a sign of decadence in art when such music is ranked with the masterpieces of German drama. But enough—the future will pronounce the verdict. . . .

127.

To Joachim.[1]

[*June* 8, 1853.]

Many thanks for your kind letter and the accompanying music; above all, for your [*Hamlet*]

[1] Schumann had known Joachim as a boy at Leipzig. They became real friends in 1853 at the Lower Rhenish musical festival, when Joachim aroused immense enthusiasm by his

overture, the very first bars of which aroused my deep interest. It was a great surprise to me to find something so very different from the gay concert overture I expected, for you had not mentioned the name of the tragedy. As I turned the pages the scene gradually rose up before me, with Ophelia and Hamlet in bodily form. There are some really impressive moments in it, and the clearness and breadth of the whole conception are proportionate to the seriousness of the task. I could say much more, but words would only imperfectly express what I feel. The music is bound to make a sympathetic impression—you may be assured of this from its effect upon me, and you make your appeal, not only to the poetic, but, in ample measure, to the purely musical sense of your hearers. The skilful interweaving of the various motifs, the new guise in which your subjects make their reappearance, and, above all, your treatment of the orchestra, particularly in obtaining original effects of light and shade, seem to me altogether admirable. There are also one or two bold transitions, extremely appropriate to the subject. . . .

Let me congratulate you on the completion of this work. Be sure you make no alterations before hearing it several times. I should very much like to have the overture for one of my first concerts.

---

performance of the Beethoven violin concerto. The friendship became even more intimate after Joachim had brought young Brahms to Düsseldorf.

Will you help to forward this by leaving us the score and the parts, if you have them?

I find my name in your handwriting on the score of the Beethoven concerto, which means, I suppose, that it is a present. I have the more pleasure in accepting it, as it reminds me of the magician who led us with perfect assurance through the mazes of this magic structure, impenetrable to most. That unforgettable day will be constantly in my thoughts when I read the concerto.

128.

To Joachim.

DÜSSELDORF, *October* 8, 1853.

. . . I think, if I were younger, I might write a few rhapsodies on the young eagle[1] who swooped down so suddenly on Düsseldorf from the Alps, or, to use another metaphor, the magnificent torrent which is at its best when, like Niagara, it dashes down as a cascade from the heights, bearing the rainbow on its surface, while its shores are haunted by the butterfly and the nightingale. I believe Johannes is another St. John the Apostle, whose revelations will puzzle many of the Pharisees, and every one else, for centuries. Only the other apostles will understand his message, including possibly Judas

[1] The dying master's enthusiastic recognition of the youthful Johannes Brahms is very touching. Worn out as Schumann was, he was the first to realize clearly the young composer's greatness. If the expression of his enthusiasm was somewhat excessive, he proved a true prophet in the main.

Iscariot, though he did not hesitate to. . . . All this is for the Apostle Joseph alone. . . .

I am sending you a new composition,[1] in which you may find reflected a certain seriousness, relieved by gleams of a lighter mood. I had you much in my mind as I wrote it, so you must be partly responsible for its character. Tell me of anything you find too difficult, for the delicacies I offer you sometimes prove to be quite uneatable dishes, or at least mouthfuls. Cross out everything that smacks of impracticability.

I could find so much more to say, but will keep it until I write again, which is as good as saying until the end of the week.

With kindest regards,

Yours,

R. SCH.

The young eagle seems quite happy on the plain. He has found an old attendant who knows from experience how to moderate the beating of the wings without injury to his flying powers. He has, besides, a faithful dog of pure German breed, who accompanies him on his daily flights, and entertains him with all sorts of jumps and tricks.

[1] Probably the Fantasia for violin and orchestra in C, Op. 131, dedicated to Joachim. [Tr.]

129.

To Joachim.

Düsseldorf, *October* 13, 1853.

I have been busy, too, just now, over four fantastic pieces for clarinet, viola, and pianoforte,[1] which now anxiously await a visit from the first violinist of the royal Hanoverian Court and State to gain them a hearing. Johannes seems very industrious. These last three days he has been practising a great deal, fired by my wife's example, perhaps. We were amazed to hear him yesterday, the difference was so great. He is capable of putting 'a girdle round about the earth in forty minutes.'

The other day I proposed a health in the form of a charade. My first was one loved by a god, my second and third one loved by many readers, and my whole, one beloved of us all. Long life to the whole in person![2]

Yours in friendship,

R. Sch.

I have begun to collect and arrange my ideas on the young eagle. Much as I should like to assist him in his first public flight, I fear that my personal attachment is too great to admit of an impartial consideration of the lights and shadows of his plumage. When I come to a conclusion, which

[1] Op. 132. [Tr.]

[2] Joachim. First syllable Io, loved of Zeus; second and third Achim (von Arnim), the romantic poet (1781-1831). [Tr.]

may be within a few days, I shall impart it to his playmate and companion-in-arms, who knows him even better than I.

October 14.

I have finished my essay, which I enclose. Please return it as soon as possible, together with the score of the concerto, as the parts have still to be copied.

130.

To Joachim.

DÜSSELDORF, *February* 6, 1854.

We have been away a whole week without sending you or your companions a sign. But I have often written to you in spirit, and there is an invisible writing, to be revealed later, underlying this letter.

I have even dreamed of you, my dear Joachim. We were spending three days together, and champagne flowed from some heron's feathers which you carried! How prosaic, but how true!

We often think of bygone days. Would we might have more like them! The friendly palace,[1] the magnificent orchestra, and the two young demons who flit backwards and forwards between them—oh! we shall not forget them.

Meanwhile I have been working at my garden,[2]

[1] In Hanover, where Joachim held an appointment.

[2] The *Poet's Garden*, a collection of criticisms of music and musicians.

which is growing more and more imposing. I have added some sign-posts, to keep people from straying —*i.e.*, an explanatory text. I am at present occupied with the ancients, Homer and the Greeks. In Plato especially I have found some splendid passages.

Music is silent for the moment—to all appearances, at least. How is it with you?

The Leipzigers have shown more sense in the matter of your *Phantasiestück*[1] than these humdrum old Rhinelanders. I think, too, that the grub, virtuosity, will gradually die, and give place to the beautiful butterfly of composition. But don't let it be too much of a black butterfly; let brighter hues have their turn. When are you going to Leipzig? Please tell me. And is the *Demetrius* overture finished?

The cigars suit me admirably. They have a Brahmsian flavour, which is strong, as usual, but agreeable. I can see a smile steal over his face!

I will close now. It is growing dark. . . .

[1] In G minor, Op. 3.

APPENDIX

THE DEEPENING TWILIGHT (1854-1856)

'I WILL close now. It is growing dark.' So the last letter ended. It was indeed growing dark in Schumann's mind, and he was soon to be compelled to lay down his life-work for ever.

Ruppert Becker, a member of the Düsseldorf orchestra, whose father had been Schumann's friend in the days of his hardest struggle, gives in his diary an account of his condition at that time. I quote from Jansen's new series of Schumann's letters (p. 533).

'*February* 14*th.*—Schumann was speaking to-day of a curious illusion of which he has been conscious for several days past. He hears inwardly exquisite musical compositions, perfect in form. The sound is generally that of distant wind-instruments, playing particularly beautiful harmonies. His inward concert actually began while we were sitting at Junge's,[1] forcing him to put away the paper he was reading. Heaven send this may mean nothing serious! So it would be, he said, in the other world, when our souls have laid aside their bodily vestment. It seems so strange that this curious

[1] A restaurant.

illusion should possess Schumann just now, when he has composed nothing for two months or more.'

'*February 21st.*—The blow of which I could not trust myself to think has fallen; Schumann has been out of his mind for some days. I only heard of it yesterday from Dietrich, who further informed me that Frau Schumann is glad when anyone comes to relieve her from her unceasing watch over him. I went to see him to-day accordingly, but should never have suspected his condition, had not Dietrich assured me of it. I found him just as usual; chatted with him for half an hour, and then took leave. Frau Schumann looks worse than I have ever seen her. If no change comes, the worst is to be feared for her. To think that in her delicate condition[1] she has not once been able to close her eyes since his illness set in. Poor, unhappy lady! She sits by the bedside all night, listening for the least movement.'

Becker saw Schumann for the last time on February 24. He writes: 'I called in the afternoon, and Frau Schumann asked me to go for a walk with him. During the hour I spent with him, he talked quite sensibly, except when he told me that Franz Schubert had appeared to him, and had played him an exquisite melody; he had, he further assured me, written this down and composed variations on it.'

When Becker returned to Düsseldorf on the 27th after one or two days' absence, he wrote: 'What

[1] She was expecting her confinement.

terrible news awaited me! Schumann stole out of his room about noon, in felt slippers, and, going straight to the Rhine, walked on to the middle of the bridge, and flung himself into the water. Happily, he had attracted attention at the entrance to the bridge by offering his silk handkerchief for toll, having no money with him. Several fishermen kept him in sight, and by pushing out in a boat, immediately after his plunge, were able to save him.'

Schumann was thereupon taken to Dr. Richarz's asylum at Endenich, near Bonn. He never left it again, although his condition lost its alarming character, and developed into an incurable weariness. The letters he wrote from there were the testimony, not of a madman, but of a sleeper lost in dreams of the past.

His love for Joachim and Brahms alone showed no falling off. Brahms, especially, repaid the kindness shown him by his faithful friendship for the invalid's wife. Clara herself never showed the true greatness of her womanhood in a higher degree than during this hard trial. Her strenuous activity and her efforts on behalf of others gave her strength and courage to live.

Robert Schumann died on July 29, 1856, at four in the afternoon.

* * * * *

I have selected from this period three letters, which will suffice to show the state of the invalid's mind. Let us rather form our estimate of him from the days of health.

131.

To his Wife.

ENDENICH, *September* 14, 1854.

How pleased I was to see your handwriting, dearest Clara.[1] Thank you for writing on this day of all days, and for your loving remembrance of me and that of the dear children. Give the little ones my love and kisses. Oh, that I could have a sight of you, a word with you all! But the distance is too great. I should be glad to know from you how you are living, and where; whether you play as gloriously as ever; whether Marie and Elise continue to make progress, and whether they still sing. Have you still the same Klemm piano? Where have my collection of (printed) scores and my manuscripts (the *Requiem*[2] and the *Sängers Fluch*,[3] for instance) been put? Where is our album with the autographs of Goethe, Jean Paul, Mozart, Beethoven, and Weber, and the various letters addressed to you and myself? Where is the *Neue Zeitschrift für Musik* and my correspondence?

[1] For six months Schumann had not asked after his wife. Suddenly, on his wedding-day (September 12), he expressed a wish to hear from her. Her letter reached him on the 13th, 'this day of all days,' her birthday.

[2] *Requiem für Mignon*, Op. 98. [Tr.]

[3] Ballad for solos, chorus, and orchestra, Op. 139, published after his death. [Tr.]

Have you still all the letters I wrote you, and the love-verses I sent to you in Paris from Vienna? Could you send me anything to read? Scherenberg's poems, for instance, some back volumes of my paper, and the *Musikalische Haus- und Lebensregeln?*[1] I also feel the want of manuscript-paper, as I sometimes feel inclined to write a little music. My life here is very simple. I take my chief pleasure in the view of Bonn, and, when I am there, in the Siebengebirge and Godesberg. You will remember sitting there in the glare of the sun, and being seized with cramp as you worked at the 'Page.'[2] I should like to know too, dear Clara, whether you have by chance sent me clothes or cigars? I particularly want to know this. Tell me more details about the children. Do they still play Beethoven, Mozart, and pieces out of my *Jugendalbum?* Does Julie keep up her playing, and how are Ludwig, Ferdinand and sweet Eugenie shaping? How I wish I could listen to your beautiful playing again! Was it all a dream—our tour in Holland last winter, your brilliant reception everywhere, particularly at Rotterdam, and the torches carried in our honour? You played the E flat concerto, Beethoven's sonatas in C major and F minor, Chopin's studies, Mendelssohn's *Songs without Words*, and my new *Konzertstück* in D in

[1] The *Advice to Young Musicians*, published as a supplement to the *Album for the Young*. [Tr.]

[2] A song of Schumann's, *Vom Pagen und der Königstochter*, Op. 140.

such glorious fashion. Do you remember how I once heard, in the night, a theme in E flat, on which I composed variations? Will you send them, and perhaps a few of your own compositions with the rest.

I am full of questions and petitions. If I could but come and voice them in person! If you think it desirable to draw a veil over any of the questions I have raised, please do so.

And now, good-bye, dearest Clara, and dear children all. Write to me soon.

Your faithful

ROBERT.

132.

ENDENICH, *September* 18, 1854.

DEAREST CLARA,

What joyful tidings you have again sent me! The birth of a fine boy—and in June,[1] too; the way in which the dear girls, Marie and Elise, celebrated your birthday by playing you the *Bilder aus Osten*[2] to your own surprise and mine; Brahms's removal to Düsseldorf for good (please give him my kindest remembrances)—these are indeed joyful tidings! If you wish to consult me in the matter of a name, you will easily guess my choice—the name of the unforgettable one.[3] I was pleased to

[1] The boy was born on June 11. Schumann's birthday was June 8.

[2] Op. 66.

[3] Mendelssohn. The boy was called Felix. He died in 1879.

hear that a complete collection of my writings, the concerto for violoncello, the fantasia for violin (which Joachim plays so magnificently), and the *Fughetten*, had been published. Can you, since you offer your services so lovingly, send me any of them? Please remember me to Joachim when you write to him. What have Brahms and Joachim been composing? Has the *Hamlet* overture made its appearance, and has he finished the other? You tell me you give your lessons in the music-room. What pupils have you now, and which are the best? Do you not find it very fatiguing, dear Clara?

8 *p.m.*—I have just returned from Bonn, where I paid my customary visit to Beethoven's statue, which always delights me. As I was standing before it, the organ in the cathedral church began to play. I am much stronger again, and look younger than I did in Düsseldorf. Now I have a request to make. Will you write and ask Dr. Peters to give me some money now and then when I want it, and let you pay it back to him? It makes me so sad to have none to give to a beggar. My life is less eventful than it was. How very different it used to be! Do tell me all about our relations and our friends in Cologne, Leipzig, Dresden and Berlin; about Woldemar[1] and Dr. Härtel—you know them all. And now let me evoke some memories for you: think of the old blissful days, of our journey to Switzerland, of

[1] Woldemar Bargiel, Clara's stepbrother.

Heidelberg, Lausanne, Chamouni; then of our visits to the Hague (where you reaped such triumphs), Antwerp, and Brussels; then of the Düsseldorf festival, with the first performance of my fourth symphony, your splendid playing, on the second day, of my A major concerto, which was so enthusiastically received, and the less enthusiastic reception of the *Rhine* overture. Do you remember, too, our first glimpse of the Alps in all their glory, and your alarm when the driver put his horse to a quick trot? I kept notes of all my journeys, including those of my school and college days, but it would give me even more pleasure if you would send me a volume of your diary, with perhaps a copy of the love-verses I sent to you in Paris from Vienna. Have you still the little double portrait, taken by Rietschel in Dresden? It would make me very happy to have it. I should also be glad to know the children's birthdays; they were written down in the little blue book.

Now I am going to write to Marie and Elise, who sent me such loving messages. So good-bye, darling Clara. Don't forget me, and write soon.

Your

ROBERT.

133.

To Johannes Brahms.

ENDENICH, *November* 27, 1854.

How I long to see you, dear friend, and hear your lovely *Variations*[1] played either by you or by Clara, of whose beautiful rendering Joachim told me in his letter. There is an exquisite coherence about the whole work, a wealth of fantastic glamour peculiarly your own, and, moreover, evidence of what is to me a new development on your part—I mean the profound skill with which you introduce the theme at odd moments, mysteriously, passionately, and again let it disappear completely. Then the wonderful close to the 14th variation, with its ingenious imitation in the second above; the 15th in G flat, with its glorious second part; and the last! Thank you, too, my dear Johannes, for all your kindness to my Clara. She speaks of it constantly in her letters. Yesterday, as perhaps you know, she sent me two volumes of my compositions and Jean Paul's *Flegeljahre*, to my great delight. I shall hope soon to see your handwriting in another sense, much as I treasure your manuscript. The winter is fairly mild. You know the neighbourhood of Bonn. I can always find pleasure in Beethoven's statue and the charming view over the Sieben-

[1] Op. 9. [Tr.]

gebirge. It was at Hanover that we last met. Be sure and write soon to your admiring and loving friend,

R. SCHUMANN.

INDEX

THE END

BILLING AND SONS, LTD., PRINTERS, GUILDFORD

CPSIA information can be obtained
at www.ICGtesting.com
Printed in the USA
LVHW101243300323
742972LV00005B/354

9 789354 008535